D0438695

Contents

Published in 2014 by Cavendish Square Publishing, LLC
303 Park Avenue South, Suite 1247, New York, NY 10010

Copyright © 2014 by Cavendish Square Publishing, LLC

First Edition

Library of Congress Cataloging-in-Publication Data

Frankel, Karen. • American Life and Fashion from Jeans to Jeggings / Karen Frankel.
p. cm. — (Pop culture) • Includes bibliographical references and index.
Summary:"Explains the importance fashion has played in post-World War II
American popular culture"—Provided by publisher.
ISBN 978-1-60870-920-5 (hardcover)—ISBN 978-1-62712-120-0 (paperback)—
ISBN 978-1-60870-925-0 (ebook)
1. Fashion design—United States—History—20th century. 2. Fashion designers—United States—
History—20th century. 3. Clothing trade—United States—History—20th century. I. Title.
TT507.F745 2013 • 746.9'2—dc23 • 2011024270

Series Consultant: Mark Mussari • Art Director: Anahid Hamparian
Series Designer: Alicia Mikles • Photo research by Lindsay Aveilhe

The photographs in this book are used by permission and through the courtesy of:

Cover photos courtesy of Everett Collection and MCT/Getty Images.
Lebrecht Music and Arts Photo Library/Alamy: p. 4; Keystone/Getty Images: p. 8; SSPL/Getty Images: p. 10; Sunset Boulevard/Corbis: p. 11; Bettmann/Corbis/AP Images: p. 13; John Springer Collection/Corbis: p. 14; AF archive/Alamy: p. 19; Paul Schutzer/Time & Life Pictures/Getty Images: p. 22; Jack Burlot/ Apis/Sygma/Corbis: p. 23; Interfoto/Alamy: p. 24; Keystone-France/Gamma-Keystone via Getty Images: p. 27; AP Photo: p. 29; Silver Screen Collection/Getty Images: p. 32; Popperfoto/Getty Images: p. 33; Leif Skoogfors/Corbis: p. 35; AF archive/Alamy: p. 37; Bettmann/Corbis: p. 38; The Advertising Archives: p. 40; Moviestore collection Ltd/Alamy: p. 42; David Montgomery/Getty Images: p. 44; Bettmann/Corbis: p. 50; Richard Howard/Time Life Pictures/Getty Images: p. 53; Pierre Guillaud/AFP/Getty Images: p. 58; Daily Mirror Mirrorpix/Newscom: p. 61; PYMCA/Alamy: p. 63; Moshe Brakha/Liaison/Getty Images: p. 66; WireImage/Getty Images: p. 67; Joe Stefanchik KRT/Newscom: p. 69; Chris Martinez/RTR/Newscom: p. 72; Louis Lanzano/AP Photo: p. 77; 20th Century Fox Film Corp./Everett Collection: p. 83; Chip Somodevilla/Getty Images: p. 87; Ramesh Sharma/India Today Group/Getty Images: p. 88.

Printed in the United States of America

POP CULTURE

American Life and Fashion from Jeans to Jeggings

KAREN FRANKEL

Cavendish Square
New York

Introduction

FASHION IS A REFLECTION OF SOCIETY AND is often change for its own sake. Fashion generally goes in a cycle—a style is innovative, has a period of popularity, and then declines, to be replaced with a new style. For generations, fashion has served to show social class and status. The "trickle-down theory of fashion" means that new styles start at the top with the wealthy and are then copied by the middle class. Once the middle class starts wearing those styles, the upper class wants something new.

For the first half of the twentieth century, France, with designers such as Coco Chanel and Christian Dior, was the fashion leader. The French developed haute couture, which literally means "high sewing." An haute couture outfit is tailored to the exact measurements of a client, and haute couture garments can cost tens of thousands of dollars, so designers also began to create prêt-a-porter (ready-to-wear) lines, which are much more affordable.

The designs of Coco Chanel dominated the fashion scene in the first half of the twentieth century.

During and following World War II, American fashion began to come into its own, although French and, also, Italian designers still set styles. While cultural influences had always been important, they began to play a much larger role in what people wore and what was considered fashionable within various segments of society. Instead of just having styles starting at the top of society, many fashions started from the bottom up. Street fashion—what is actually being worn on the street—became a major factor in determining what was "in" during the 1960s. By the 1970s, trend designers, whose collections portray a certain look, such as "preppy" or "classic," became important.

Fashion, whether it came from the top down, from the bottom up, or from trend collections, intermixed with popular culture, from movies and television, to art and literary movements. Social mores and concerns, ethnic identity, sports, economics, politics, and technology were also factors in determining what was fashionable. In some cases, culture influenced fashion, while in others, fashion influenced the culture. The process goes back and forth, from pop culture to fashion and then back to pop culture. Sometimes, while there's no discernible relationship, it's interesting to try and figure out what the connection might be.

1950s:
Post-War America and the Age of Conformity

DURING WORLD WAR II, FASHION WAS PUT on the back burner as most of the nation's resources were directed toward the war effort. The U.S. government restricted the amount and types of fabric that could be used for clothing. This meant, for example, that men's pants couldn't have pleats or cuffs because that would use too much fabric.

Nylon, which was invented in the 1930s by American chemical company Du Pont, had begun to replace silk for women's stockings, which at the time were made with seams running down the back of the leg. However, all the nylon available was required by the government for parachutes and other military items. To make it look as though they were still wearing stockings, women began putting on leg make-up and painting their own seams down the backs of their legs.

POST-WAR TRENDS

When the war ended, thousands of veterans, known as GIs (short for Government Issue), came home. The GI Bill, passed in 1944, helped veterans receive higher education and job training and guaranteed loans for homes, farms, and businesses. For

World War II created a shortage in both fabric and nylon. Dresses got shorter and narrower, and women took to painting stocking seams down the backs of their legs.

the first time, college and homeownership became possibilities for the average American. GIs married, started families, and moved to the suburbs. And they came home to a "New Look" in women's fashion.

French designer Christian Dior introduced the "New Look" in 1947. Dior's fashions featured long, wide skirts that went to mid-calf, tiny waists, and natural shoulders. It was a very different look from the clothes women had worn during the war: suits that were influenced by military uniforms, with wide shoulders and knee-length hems, blouses with shoulder pads, and pants for working in factories. With the New Look, skirts could use as much as 25 to 30 yards of fabric, an enormous amount, especially when compared to wartime restrictions that allowed only 1-3/4 yards to make a dress. The New Look was a huge success, seeming just right after years of fabric rationing and the masculine style of women's clothes that was prominent during the war. Women across the United States seemed eager to embrace the new style.

Dior said, "No one person can change fashion—a big fashion change imposes itself. It was because women longed to look like women again that they adopted the New Look." However, Dior represented the power of the French haute couture designers who influenced so many 1950s styles. After the New Look, Dior introduced his pencil line in 1948. It had narrow skirts that were so tight they required a slit in the material to allow women to walk. His H-line, brought out in 1954 and named for the silhouette of the garment, evolved into his A-line in 1955, which looks like the shape of the letter A with its narrow shoulders and wide hem.

WOMEN'S FASHION AND 1950S SOCIETY

The fashions of the 1950s reflected the various roles women played. Many women, who had worked on farms and in factories during the war, returned to their traditional roles as housewives and mothers. As wives, they were expected to help their husbands' careers by dressing appropriately, and looking pretty and feminine at all times. The wife/mother look was conservative, featuring shirtwaist-style dresses, full skirts with crinolines, and high heels. Gloves were part of the dress code required for almost all occasions. Pants were only considered appropriate for women at informal occasions or at home, and the style was for toreador or capri pants, which have narrow legs and end mid-calf.

During World War II, women entered the workforce in droves as men were serving in the military. In the post-war years, women retreated to the home front, and femininity in attire and attitude ruled the roost.

A different look and role for women was that of the femme fatale, represented by Marilyn Monroe, whose tight outfits emphasized her seductive appeal. To accentuate, or even create, the smooth curves necessary to achieve the desired look, women wore constricting undergarments. (They also needed these undergarments to achieve the New Look's wasp waist.) The merry widow, a foundation garment with hooks or zippers in the front or laces in the back, went from the bust to the hips, providing support for the breasts, and giving women a nipped-in waist. For the "sweater girl" look that made Hollywood starlets into sex symbols and pin-up girls, women chose

The femme fatale look was a counterpoint to the happy housewife image. It was best embodied by Marilyn Monroe, particularly in 1950s films such as *Gentlemen Prefer Blondes*.

bras with cone-shaped cups that emphasized the breasts, especially when worn under a tight sweater. Girdles, which went from the waist to the upper thighs, held stockings up and gave a smooth look to the stomach and rear.

Separates—interchangeable skirts, tops, and pants that extended a woman's wardrobe at a lower cost than buying several complete outfits—also became popular. Separates reflected the more active lifestyle of American women and were the mainstay of the American ready-to-wear market. Ready-to-wear clothes are mass-produced and can be bought off the rack at stores, as opposed to high-end custom-made clothes that are fitted to an individual's body. Designers Bonnie Cashin, Anne Klein, and Claire McCardell (who is sometimes called the "Mother of American Fashion") were known for their "American Look" collections, with styles more casual than those of French designers. New York and California designers, as well as costume designers for movies, had promoted sporty American styles since the 1930s.

In the mid–1950s, the sack dress, or chemise, was introduced by Spanish couturier Cristóbal Balenciaga and French designers Hubert de Givenchy and Christian Dior. With its unfitted style, the chemise was almost the total opposite of the New Look. Givenchy said that it was "inspired by modern art." The chemise in turn inspired several pop and Doo-wop songs in 1958, including "No Chemise, Please," by Gerry Granahan, "Bobbin' in a Sack" by the Lane Brothers, and the "Sack Dress" by the Beavers. It's a perfect example of how fashion and pop culture influence each other—from modern art to fashion to pop music.

Women's fashion was also influenced by one specific social occasion—the cocktail party—which led to the popularity of the cocktail dress. These dresses were made of silk, velvet, or brocade and were much dressier than day dresses, though

Fashion designers such as Claire McCardell became known for outfits such as this one, which emphasized the sportier look of the American female.

not as elegant as floor-length evening gowns. They often had a full or balloon skirt. The bodice had thin spaghetti straps and showed a certain amount of décolleté. A matching short jacket might also be worn.

MEN'S FASHIONS

After the war, men looked forward to being the breadwin-ners, working for large corporations as they supported their families. *The Man in the Gray Flannel Suit*, a novel about corpo-rate life, sums up the look for men during the 1950s—suits with a single-breasted three-button charcoal gray jacket and trousers with no pleats. Shirts were white or pale blue with a button-down collar. Men usually wore fedoras or snap-brim hats year round.

Gregory Peck (*center*) stands on a commuter train platform in this still from the 1956 film, *The Man in the Gray Flannel Suit*, which highlighted the constant pressures to conform in all aspects of life, including dress.

The 1950s was a period of fashion conformity for men's dress. Even in casual wear, men dressed alike. Tweed jackets with gray flannel slacks were the favored style for conservative dressers, while other men picked sports jackets in colorful madras plaids. Hawaiian print shirts could be seen at informal occasions, especially barbecuing in the back yard. Bermuda shorts were also popular, and some American men followed the custom on the island of Bermuda of wearing the shorts with knee-length socks.

1950S TELEVISION AND FASHION

Television had a major impact on American fashion. For the first time, people from different parts of the country could see on a daily basis what anchors of national news broadcasts or hosts of variety shows were wearing. Television provided an instant view of what was "in." Because there were only a few networks in those days, which limited program choice, what was in was the same everywhere. The nation had a unified dress code.

Television programs such as *Father Knows Best, Leave It to Beaver,* and *The Adventures of Ozzie & Harriet* reinforced traditional family roles and traditional fashion. These programs, along with others like them, portrayed idealized versions of middle-class families. The TV mothers wore tight-fitting, full-skirted shirtwaist dresses, heels, stockings, and jewelry; the fathers wore suits or conservative casual clothes. Even women in commercials wore high heels and a string of pearls. The concept of at-home clothes to watch television emerged, and stay-at-home slippers, mules, and sandals became part of a woman's wardrobe.

TV cowboys and cowgirls, from Roy Rogers and Dale Evans to Walt Disney's Davy Crockett, made the frontier look a fashion staple for youngsters. A Dale Evans outfit was made up of a fringed vest, blouse with a fancy yoke, guns, holsters, and boots. It was at the top of many girls' holiday wish lists, while boys wanted to look like their favorite cowboys with hats, chaps, and cowboy shirts.

In 1954 and 1955, Walt Disney broadcast the story of *Davy Crockett, King of the Wild Frontier.* Starring Fess Parker, the three-episode series was a huge hit, and it started the craze for coonskin hats and fringed leather jackets that swept the nation. Every kid wanted his or her own piece of Davy Crockett mania and $100 million worth of three thousand different items, from lunchboxes to jackets, were sold.

AMERICAN BANDSTAND

For teenagers, *American Bandstand* was the hip afternoon program in the late 1950s. The show premiered nationwide on ABC in August 1957 with Dick Clark as host. It featured Philadelphia teens, mostly from working-class families, doing every type of dance, from the twist to the jitterbug, the cha-cha, and slow dances, while rock-and-roll performers and stars made guest appearances. The show also provided a front-seat view of the *Bandstand* "in" fashions. The look for girls: full skirts with hoops and crinolines, straight skirts paired with sweaters, princess-line dresses (which were dresses that had a flared skirt and no seam at the waist), black flats with stockings, sneakers with white socks, and bouffant hair-dos. The dress code for boys required a jacket or sweater with a tie. Jeans were not allowed.

TEENAGE IDOLS

During the 1950s, for the first time in history, clothes were made specifically with teenagers in mind. Teens no longer had to wear junior versions of their parents' outfits. Magazines such as *Seventeen*, as well as manufacturers and department stores, helped promote the teen fashions of the day.

Many teenagers adopted one of two basic looks: preppy or greaser. The preppy look was named after the "prep" or "preparatory boarding schools" that affluent teens attended instead of public high schools in order to prepare them for college. For boys, the casual preppy look included tweed sports coats, crew neck or V-neck sweaters, and oxford cloth button-down shirts. Their shoes were penny loafers or white bucks—which were made popular by singer and teen idol Pat Boone. Their hair was cut in short, military-style crew cuts or flattops. For a crew cut, an electric razor is used, following the contour of the head, while a flat-top is similar to a crew cut, but the hair on the top of the head is cut and styled to stand up straight, making the top appear flat. Girls would wear sweater sets, circle or poodle skirts (skirts cut in a circle, often with a poodle or other appliqué attached near the hemline), skirts with lots of petticoats or crinolines underneath to give a full, bell-like appearance, saddle shoes, and bobby socks. Casual wear sometimes consisted of an oversized white shirt with rolled-up jeans.

The greaser or "hood" look came from the rock-and-roll subculture, which was just beginning in the 1950s. Elvis Presley, with his slick, combed-back hairstyle that required grease or hair cream to keep it in place, was one of the major influences. Marlon Brando, who starred in the movie *The Wild One*, and James Dean, the star of the film *Rebel Without a Cause*, were both models for greasers as well. Greasers wore tight blue jeans, T-shirts with rolled-up sleeves for storing a pack of cigarettes, and leather motorcycle jackets. Footwear was either biker boots or dark-colored loafers with white socks. Sideburns were popular among greasers, as were ducktails, a longish hair style in which the hair at the back of the neck was cut to resemble the tail feathers on a duck. Girls wore heavy make-up, tight sweaters, and short skirts.

The greaser look was an act of rebellion against society, and because society at large equated juvenile delinquency with rock-and-roll fashion, dress codes were imposed at many schools. These codes called for boys to wear shirts and ties, standard trousers or khakis (no jeans), and polished shoes, while girls could wear skirts, jumpers, dresses, blouses, sweaters, and jackets (no pants).

BEATS AND FASHION: THE COUNTERCULTURE OF THE 1950S

One influential group from the late 1940s through the 1950s were the Beats—a small group of writers, including novelists Jack Kerouac (*On the Road*), William S. Burroughs (*Naked Lunch*), and poet Allen Ginsberg (*Howl*). They believed in freedom of expression and spontaneity. Their tastes ran to improvisational bebop jazz, abstract expressionist art, mind-altering drugs, and "free love." They broke the rules of the conformist society of the 1950s, from the way people were supposed to dress to how they lived.

As with many subcultures, dress was a means of identification. A beatnik stereotype emerged. Young women, or "chicks," had long straight hair and dressed in black leotards, turtlenecks, or men's shirts over slacks or jeans. Black stretch pants with stirrups and black ballet slippers were another option. Men, or "cats," wore black turtlenecks or worn shirts, faded jeans, berets, horn-rimmed glasses, and had goatees. Dark glasses were a favored accessory both indoors and out.

In 1957, the film *Funny Face* starred Audrey Hepburn as a beatnik who wore a black sweater, long black stockings, and black slacks when she worked in a bookstore in New York City's Greenwich Village. In August 1959, *Life* printed a fashion spread entitled "Real Gone Garb for Fall, Beat but Neat," which showed how "unbeat beat clothing is becoming." The spread featured loose sweaters paired with tight black trousers, skirts, and leotards. Beat fashion had become almost mainstream for college students, especially young intellectuals, who wanted to identify with the Beats.

In *Funny Face*, Audrey Hepburn played a beatnik who gets a make-over when she is discovered by a fashion photographer. The movie was based on the real-life story of Doe and Richard Avedon.

FASHION ICON
AUDREY HEPBURN

Audrey Hepburn was one of the most popular movie stars during the 1950s and 1960s, as well as a fashion icon throughout her life. In *Breakfast at Tiffany's* (1961) Hepburn wore a black cocktail dress designed by French couturier Hubert de Givenchy. The dress became known as the "little black dress." Hepburn wore Givenchy creations in several of her films, as well as in her personal wardrobe. Known for her simple, spare style, Hepburn was the epitome of chic.

FASHION FABRICS

Synthetic fabrics including Orlon, an acrylic, and Dacron, a polyester, started replacing natural fibers such as cotton, linen, and wool. "Better living through chemistry" was the DuPont Company's slogan, and for 1950s housewives and teenagers, better living meant easy care with wash-and-wear clothes. It seemed as though spending hours ironing crisp cotton blouses was going to become a task of the past, especially when synthetics and synthetic blends became popular. However, clothes made of natural fibers later came back into style, guaranteeing the continued use of the iron and ironing board.

DECADE IN REVIEW

During World War II, the United States had been isolated from the French fashion influence, thus giving American designers and fashion a chance to come into their own. But in the post-war era, French designers returned to their former prominence and the American fashion magazines that many women relied on for their fashion advice highlighted the styles that the French couture designers created.

The new way of life in the United States, with its middle-class suburbs and outdoor activities, helped popularize casual dress. Still, traditional attire—dresses for women and suits for men—remained the norm for most occasions.

With the exception of those movements that rebelled against the status quo, specifically the Beats and the rock-and-roll subculture that inspired the greaser look, 1950s fashions reflected the desire for conformity. Television reinforced traditional family roles and conservative clothing, but it also aided in the acceptance of new types of dress for teenagers, and encouraged fads. These teenagers and their baby boomer siblings (people born from 1946 to 1964) would turn the 1960s into a youth revolution from politics to fashion.

TWO

1960s:
The Times Are Changing

THE 1960S WERE A TIME OF CHANGE AND protest, including the civil rights movement, the creation of the National Organization for Women (NOW), and increasing dissent over the war in Vietnam. But the decade started off by introducing one of the twentieth century's most famous fashion icons, Jacqueline Kennedy.

POLITICS AND FASHION

The wife of the youngest president in U.S. history, First Lady Jackie Kennedy set trends such as pillbox hats, shifts, A-line dresses, casual slacks, chic T-shirts, sunglasses, and even bouffant hair. During the 1960 presidential campaign, she was criticized for her patronage of French designers, so after the election, she worked with U.S. designer Oleg Cassini to create new outfits. Their designs were then copied by millions of American women. Jackie often wore crisp suits with a semi-fitted jacket that ended just above the hipbone. Her skirts hit at mid-knee or just below. Her dresses and tops were often sleeveless.

President John F. Kennedy had his own impact on fashion. Hat sales dropped after Kennedy went without one at his 1961

At an inaugural event for her husband, new First Lady Jacqueline Kennedy wore a dress designed by Oleg Cassini. Soon the entire world seemed to be wearing . . . whatever Jackie wore!

inauguration, and by the end of the decade, the trend of wearing hats every day for businessmen had disappeared.

In a special address to Congress in his first year in office, President Kennedy made a commitment to land an American on the moon by the end of the decade. On July 20, 1969, during President Richard Nixon's administration, Commander Neil Armstrong became the first man to walk on the moon. But, "space age" fashion and make-up had already entered the scene.

French designer André Courrèges's 1964 Space Age Collection for women included white catsuits and silver "moon girl" trousers. The Courrèges look also included white kidskin boots with a flat heel (which became known as go-go boots), sleeveless or short-sleeved minidresses, and square-cut tunics.

As the 1960s went on, society became freer, and so did fashion. French designer André Courreges (*third from left*) is shown here surrounded by models in trend-setting clothes.

The collection was such a success that it influenced designers Pierre Cardin and Paco Rabanne to create their own versions. Rabanne's fashions used plastic squares attached to fabric backings and Cardin's streamlined apparel featured "cutout" round holes. Cardin also dressed men and women alike in unitards and jumpsuits.

American designers also played a part in the space age trend. Betsey Johnson made clear vinyl minidresses that came with decals the buyer could use for decoration. Rudi Gernreich added clear vinyl panels on both his minidresses and bathing suits.

Cosmetic manufacturers followed the trend by advertising their frosted lipsticks as "moon babies," saying "New silver-

23

sizzled pales with a sheen never seen on Earth before." Hairstyles took a modern turn as well, going from the elaborate beehive and bouffant looks of the early 1960s to short, geometric styles inspired by hair stylist Vidal Sassoon.

FASHION AND FINE ART

From Piet Mondrian to Andy Warhol, the art world became notably intertwined with fashion in the mid–1960s. Yves Saint Laurent's 1965 straight jersey dresses, divided by strips of color into squares and rectangles, were directly influenced by the geometric paintings of Piet Mondrian, a Dutch abstractionist.

Some of the most interesting fashions of the 1960s were influenced by fine art, such as this dress that mimics Piet Mondrian's paintings.

Pop artist Andy Warhol's work was featured in fashion as well. He created silk screens of celebrities, paintings of every-day items like Campbell's soup cans, and wooden sculptures that replicated the cardboard supermarket cartons of products like Brillo soap pads. Copies of his work could be seen on various pieces of clothing. One example is "The Souper Dress," a paper dress printed with the pattern of a Campbell's soup can. Warhol inspired a number of designers, including Yves Saint Laurent, who based his 1966 pop art collection on Warhol's work, as well as that of pop artist Tom Wesselman. Saint Laurent used the curves of the body as a way "to break up the linear, geometric shapes of the dresses."

Op artists Victor Vasarely and Bridget Riley also influenced fashion. Op art gives the illusion of three-dimensional movement and was the inspiration for the cutouts in Cardin's Space Age collection. Rudi Gernreich extended op art patterns from his dresses to the shoes and stockings to create a total look.

Both op and pop art appeared on paper dresses, which were a fad in the late 1960s. These simple, short shifts could be worn several times and then discarded. Inexpensive, with eye-catching patterns, paper dresses were called the "ultimate smart-money fashion" by *Mademoiselle* in June 1967.

THE MINISKIRT: SYMBOL OF THE 1960S

Probably no article of clothing says the 1960s quite like the miniskirt. Though French designer André Courrèges showed miniskirts in his 1964 collection, it was British designer Mary Quant who popularized them. Quant noticed that young girls in England were wearing short skirts, anywhere from two to nine inches above the knee, and put them in her collection. The miniskirt is an example of how street fashion has influenced the fashion industry. Along with the miniskirt, the London look included patterned stockings, tight-ribbed sweaters, and tall go-go boots, made of vinyl or leather. Because of the shortness of the skirt, it was impossible to wear garter belts and thigh-high stockings, which were traditionally worn by women under skirts and dresses. Tights, or the new pantyhose, went up to the waist, which meant there was no need for a girdle or garter belt to hold up the stockings. Quant's clothes and the London look were featured in *Seventeen* and quickly caught on with American teens.

In the midst of the miniskirt craze, two new movies gave young women an alternative to short skirts. In 1967, the movie *Bonnie and Clyde* started another fashion trend. Faye Dunaway's gangster glamour girl Bonnie wore Depression-era slinky "midi-skirts," twin sets, and berets. The other film, *Doctor Zhivago*, was described as a love story "caught in the fire of a revolution," when it was released in 1965. Set in the era surrounding the Russian Revolution, *Doctor Zhivago*'s popularity lasted for years and helped inspire long coats, fur hats, and high boots, which first appeared in the mid–1960s and then again in the 1970s. The reappearance of a fashion is called a "retro" trend. Styles of past generations are often recycled. The original clothing from the period is called vintage.

THE BRITISH INVASION

Mary Quant's miniskirt was only one aspect of the British invasion of the 1960s. In 1964, the Beatles arrived in New York and made a huge impression on men's fashion as well as on music. The Beatles "mop top," long hair with bangs, was copied by many young men. The Beatles wore matching collarless suits, with short, fitted jackets and skinny tapered pants that reflected the Mod look of London's swinging Carnaby Street, three blocks full of modern boutiques.

The Mod look, short for modern, turned menswear from staid and sober to colorful and bold. Though the Mod style

The Beatles rocked fashion for men, though their strongest influence was on hair. After the Beatles popped onto the American scene, long—and ever longer—hair became the fashion for men for years.

began in Britain, it soon became an international fad. The Mods paid attention to every detail of their clothes. In addition to the Beatles, Rod "the Mod" Stewart, and members of several bands, including The Who led by Pete Townshend, wore the look. The Beatles moved from Mod style to shirts in vivid psychedelic

27

tones and suits with paisley prints. On the cover of their album *Sgt. Pepper's Lonely Hearts Club Band* (1967), the band wore old-fashioned stand-up collar military uniforms in acid green, cerulean blue, hot pink, and cadmium red, with contrasting colored braids. Their new style was part of the Peacock Revolution, a term coined by *Esquire* columnist George Frazier to describe the flamboyant men's fashions. Other men's magazines, such as *Playboy* and *GQ*, encouraged this new look.

As the Beatles and other prominent musicians began exploring Eastern religions, some began wearing the Nehru jacket, named after the former Indian prime minister who had worn them. The jacket is collarless and single-breasted, and it was often paired with a turtleneck and love beads. Where the pop musicians led, fashion, at least for young men and women, followed.

THE HIPPIE MOVEMENT

In January 1967, thousands of hippies from across the country gathered at Golden Gate Park in San Francisco. Hippies, like the Beats the decade before, were part of a counterculture movement and they adopted many of the same ideas and causes. These ranged from Eastern religion, pacifism, and environmental concerns to gay rights, free love, and recreational drug use, including marijuana and hallucinogens such as LSD.

The hippie look, which is often called antifashion, was a rejection of contemporary fashion and technological advances. Synthetic fibers and plastics were cast aside in favor of natural fibers. Blue jeans, often hand-embroidered with flowers, were a symbol of hippie culture for both sexes. "Flower power" was a slogan that came from the flowers hippies would insert in the rifle barrels of the military at anti-war protests. At the Woodstock Music and Art Festival in Bethel, New York, in August 1969, some 450,000 young people came to hear rock musicians

Ironically, the hippie "antifashion" look quickly became the height of fashion for a generation.

such as Janis Joplin, Jimi Hendrix, and Jefferson Airplane. The attendees' dress was typical of the way many teens in the United States dressed at the time. Many wore unisex clothing such as T-shirts and bell-bottomed jeans. Long hair was common on both men and women, along with love beads, tie-dyed clothing, peace symbols, and protest buttons. Many men had beards and mustaches.

Hippies believed that each person should create his or her own individual style, but in reality, several looks became prominent. Some hippies went for the ethnic look, which incorporated long, printed, cotton skirts from India, African dashikis (collarless tunics with kimono-style sleeves, usually in bright colors—worn by men), fringed jackets and vests, and beaded headbands like those worn by American Indians.

Others went for the international peasant look, wearing ponchos, Peruvian wool hats, and Afghani sheepskin jackets.

Many hippies wore second-hand clothing and often made their own clothes. Crocheted halter tops, tie-dyed scarves and T-shirts, patchwork, embroidery, and macramé reinforced the do-it-yourself, or DIY, philosophy.

BLACK POWER

Several pieces of civil rights legislation were passed in the 1960s, but progress for equal rights was often slow. While Martin Luther King Jr. preached nonviolent action, other black leaders, such as black power advocate Stokely Carmichael and Nation of Islam minister Malcolm X, didn't always agree with a nonviolent approach. The Black Panther Party, a group that advocated violence against the power structure as a way to achieve a socialist state, had its own style of dress: a uniform of blue shirts or black turtleneck sweaters, black pants, black leather jackets, and black berets for both men and women.

The Afro hairstyle became a symbol of black power as well as a symbol of the "black is beautiful" cultural movement that encouraged African Americans to take pride in their looks. Afro-ethnic clothing became popular during the 1960s and 1970s. For men, the clothes included dashikis, caftans (a floor-length dashiki), and djellabas (a long robe with a hood). Women wore batik wrap skirts, Yoruba-style head wraps (turbans), large hooped earrings, and cowrie shell jewelry.

THE NEW MORALITY

In addition to music and fashion, the 1960s brought changes in social and sexual values. Previously, it was almost unheard of for young middle-class men and women to live together before marriage, although the 1953 Kinsey Report indicated that half of the women in its study had had sex before marriage. Nevertheless, the prospect of becoming pregnant kept many women from engaging in sexual activity. But when the Federal Drug Administration approved the birth control pill in 1960, sexual liberation began.

At first, doctors would only prescribe birth control pills to married women, and some states made it illegal to prescribe them to single women. But it wasn't long before "the Pill," as it became known, made a huge difference in sexual behavior and mores among young men and women, as well as in the way women envisioned their choices and obligations. With a nonintrusive, dependable means of contraception, new options were available for both single and married women. Life could include both a family and a career. The Equal Pay Act of 1963 and Title VII of the Civil Rights Act in 1964 (which prohibited discrimination in employment on the basis of sex as well as race, religion, and national origin), were the first small steps toward workplace equality.

Women's fashion reflected the sexual liberation movement. What was socially acceptable in women's dress changed drastically during the decade. Bikinis, for example, came into mainstream fashion. Although bikinis had been seen on the beaches of St. Tropez in France, and were worn by French film stars such as Brigitte Bardot, they didn't start gaining acceptance in the United States until the 1960s.

The song "Itsy Bitsy Teenie Weenie Yellow Polka Dot Bikini," which made wearing the new swimsuit seem like fun, hit the charts in 1960. Beach movies, such as *Beach Party* (1963), showed teenagers, including former Mouseketeer Annette Funicello, wearing them. James Bond movies often featured "Bond girls" in skimpy swimwear. In 1964, Rudi Gernreich pushed the boundaries by introducing his monokini, a topless bathing suit. The no-bra look became popular. Women began wearing soft, nonstructured bras instead of the cone-shaped

As the 1960s wore on, the teensy bikini became common beachwear.

bras of the 1950s. By the end of the decade, going braless was common among many teens and women. For some the choice was about comfort, but for others it was a statement protesting conformity. Fashion magazines had a test for deciding whether a young woman could go braless: if a pencil placed below the breast fell to the ground, going without a bra was okay, but many women ignored such guidelines.

Men's magazines, including *Playboy*, *GQ*, and *Esquire*, also promoted the new morality with its open sexuality, as well as their regular articles and photo spreads on the latest fashions for men.

FASHION FACES OF THE 1960S

British models Jean Shrimpton and Twiggy were among the best-known faces of the 1960s. Their images reflected a change from the 1950s fashion models, who exemplified the ladylike, sophisticated look, to those who represented the youthful, counterculture style of the 1960s. Shrimpton was involved with photographer David Bailey. (The 1966 movie *Blow-Up* about a London photographer is believed to be based on him.) Twiggy, a London teenager with short hair and long eyelashes, epitomized the new look of the 1960s. Born Leslie Hornby, the nickname Twiggy reflected her super-slim, boyish figure, a look that returned to popularity in the 1990s with model Kate Moss.

Some believe that Twiggy, thus named because she was so slender and boyish, started the modern-day female obsession with weight loss. It definitely changed the look of the female model.

DECADE IN REVIEW

The 1960s were a time of upheaval in politics, culture, and social values, with the civil rights movement, the Vietnam War, and the introduction of the birth control pill. Between the 1950s and the 1960s the concept of the ideal women's figure changed dramatically. For many in the 1950s, screen star Marilyn Monroe, with her voluptuous body, was the desired female image. In 1959, when the Barbie doll was introduced, it had an idealized women's silhouette with curves and a tiny waist. Twiggy, the teenage model who became a style icon in the 1960s, had an almost androgynous appearance, slim body, and childlike looks.

In the 1960s, fashion trends came from the top down with Jackie Kennedy and her fondness for styles by name designers and from the bottom up with the miniskirt and the hippie look as prime examples of street fashion. Fun clothes, whether they were disposable paper dresses or the high fashion couture look inspired by the art world or the space race, helped give the 1960s their sense of youth and fun.

Politics, ethnicity, and the breakdown of conventions helped splinter the 1950s conservative conformity of fashion. Each segment of the population found its own way to express itself through dress. This quest for self-expression continued through the early years of the 1970s, with 1960s fashion playing a major part.

THREE

1970s:
The "Me" Generation

WITH THE WAR IN VIETNAM STILL RAGING, the protests of the 1960s continued into the early 1970s. Both hippies and war protesters influenced fashion trends with unisex clothing, including jeans, cotton T-shirts, tank tops, and boots staying popular. The counterculture film *Easy Rider* (1969) featured motorcycle-riding hippie dropouts as the main characters.

The Vietnam War had a profound effect on the nation. It also influenced fashion, with some antiwar protestors wearing slightly altered military garb.

Actor Peter Fonda wore a leather jacket with the American flag on the back, while actor/director Dennis Hopper wore a Western-style fringed jacket and either a cowboy hat or headband. Both men wore their hair long; Fonda sported sideburns, and Hopper, a bushy mustache.

Hippies continued to reject the consumerism of their parents and society at large. DIY was a major trend in the early 1970s. Handmade crocheted vests and caps, knitted shawls, and batik shirts remained popular. Jeans were flared or bell-bottomed, and combining faded blue jeans with an Indian tunic was a prominent look.

Politics also influenced clothing. The first official Earth Day to save the environment was held in 1970. Growing concerns about the environment made natural fibers preferable among young people. The women's liberation movement also gained momentum. *Ms.* magazine was founded in 1971 by a group of feminists, including outspoken journalist and activist Gloria Steinem, providing a national voice to the movement. To show their support of feminist ideas, many young women moved away from clothing they considered sexist, such as high heels, tight skirts, and bras.

In fact, the 1970s started with a rejection of what the Paris designers were offering: long skirts. Although the trend of long coats began in 1968, skirts were still worn short. So when Paris designers introduced midis (skirts and dresses with a hemline that was mid-calf), American women said no. Hemlines did drop gradually over time, coming to a little below the knee. Young women turned to floor-length "granny" dresses, often featuring Laura Ashley flower prints. But the real fashion revolution during the 1970s was the way pants took over in women's clothing. The 1970s were the first time that pants were considered acceptable for women's wear in the office as well as for informal occasions and by students in school.

THE RISE AND FALL OF HEMLINES

In the 1920s, economist George Taylor suggested that hemlines go up in times of prosperity and down during economic recessions. According to Taylor, women raise their hemlines to show off their expensive silk stockings in good economic times, and lower their hemlines when times are bad to hide the fact they aren't wearing stockings. The hemline theory isn't true, according to fashion historian Valerie Steele. She wrote, "Although superficially plausible," the stock market's ups and down during the 1970s didn't correspond to a "rise and fall of hemlines."

As the battle for civil rights continued, Afro-ethnic styles and clothing moved from the streets into the designer world. Although Afros were very fashionable, cornrows—rows of very tight braids—were also worn by African Americans, including celebrities such as actress Cicely Tyson and musician Rick James. In the 1979 movie *10*, actress Bo Derek wore her hair in cornrows and the style became briefly popular with white women.

When Bo Derek wore her hair in cornrows in the movie *10*, she sparked a brief craze for the hairdo among white women and a continuing one for women of color.

Young black designer Stephen Burrows, whose super-bright jersey knits and use of black models impressed the fashion world, was one of five designers chosen to represent American style at a fashion show supporting the restoration of the palace at Versailles, France, in 1973. The other four designers were Bill Blass, Anne Klein, Oscar de la Renta, and Halston. The five designers representing France at the show were Yves Saint Laurent, Christian Dior, Hubert de Givenchy, Emanuel Ungaro, and Pierre Cardin. According to *Women's Wear Daily, 100 Years*, "Americans Conquer Versailles." It was the moment when American fashion arrived.

African American designer Stephen Burrows became famous for his super-bright, hand-painted, flowing fashions.

JEANS

Jeans are made of denim, a cloth that was originally called "serge de Nîmes," which means serge or twill fabric from the city of Nimes, France. It's easy to see how the French *"de Nîmes"* turned into the English word "denim."

During the California Gold Rush of 1849, tailor Jacob Davis made denim work pants for the gold prospectors. He bought the denim from Levi Strauss, the owner of a wholesale fabric supply house in San Francisco. Davis used copper rivets to reinforce the pockets that kept ripping out from frequent use. Davis was worried that competitors might steal his design, so he wanted to patent it. He asked Levi Strauss for the $68 filing fee for the patent. In return, he offered Strauss a half interest in the product, and Levi's came into being.

Indigo, a natural blue dye that is colorfast—which means it does not run or bleed onto other fabric—was used for the denim cloth, and the pants became known as "blue jeans." The name jeans comes from the denim pants that working people had worn in Europe since the seventeenth century, even though that denim was a different fabric than the one used by Levi Strauss. That fabric was made in Genoa, Italy, and the French name for the city was "Gênes," which sounds close to the English word "jeans."

Strauss kept making improvements to the jeans, adding logos and introducing new styles, such as the overalls—jeans with a bib—and a version for women. Other companies, including Lee and Wrangler, also started making jeans.

While used mostly as men's work pants, jeans got a bit of glamour when Hollywood put cowboys in them. Then, in the 1930s, teenage girls started to wear jeans for informal occasions.

In the 1950s, jeans became a symbol of rebellion. And, by the 1960s, they were the favored wear of hippies, war protestors, and teenagers everywhere. Jeans were embroidered, painted, studded, and appliquéd. In 1969, the Gap was founded in San Francisco as a store entirely devoted to jeans. At first, the Gap sold only Levi's jeans but by 1975 it sold its own Gap brands.

By the 1970s, jeans were an international phenomenon. Americans traveling abroad wearing jeans were asked if they wanted to sell them. In 1973, Levi Strauss received the Neiman Marcus Fashion Award for "the single most important American contribution to worldwide fashion."

Jeans became highly fashion when companies like Gloria Vanderbilt, Pierre Cardin, Jordache, and Calvin Klein produced designer blue jeans. One of the most popular and racy advertisements of 1980 featured Brooke Shields wearing a pair of Calvin Klein jeans saying, "Want to know what gets between me and my Calvins? Nothing."

Jeans became popular with teens in the 1960s and 1970s as an anti-fashion statement, but Brooke Shields made jeans sexy and sought after in the 1980s.

Today, denim may be stone-washed, shrunk, faded, or bleached in styles such as bell-bottoms, boot cuts, or relaxed fit. They may be hip-huggers, low-cut, or have a natural waist, and the colors range from white to black to any shade in between. In 2010, jeggings—leggings that appeared to be jeans with fake pockets and zippers—became the rage.

Jeans—in all their variations—have become the American classic.

THE EXERCISE BOOM

Nike was launched in 1972 as an athletic shoe company, and not long after, its swoosh logo became world famous. By 1978, sales of running shoes accounted for 50 percent of all shoes sold in the United States. Whether Americans were actually athletes or just wanted to look like them, wearing athletic shoes became one of the biggest fashion trends of the decade. The warm-up suit, according to *Sports Illustrated*, was one of the hottest fashions around in 1972. Worn by both men and women, warm-up suits in a multitude of colors appeared everywhere. In 1976, Olympic figure skater Dorothy Hamill started another trend as her wedge-shaped haircut was copied by millions of young girls and women.

Americans were becoming more active, taking up jogging and joining health clubs. People wanted to show off bodies that were toned by exercise, and bodysuits made that possible. Bodysuits were made of Lycra, the trade name for spandex, a stretch fiber developed by DuPont in the 1960s. Lycra was blended with cotton, wool, silk, and other synthetics in leggings and leotards to make activewear fashionable as well as functional.

Weekend athletes went for the outdoor sportsperson look. Outdoor clothes and shoes from two long-established companies, Eddie Bauer, which introduced the first quilted down jacket, and L. L. Bean, a Maine manufacturer known for its mail-order catalog, came into vogue.

MUSIC MAKES FASHION

DISCO

Discotheques, commonly called discos, were the nightclubs of the 1970s. With disk jockeys playing the latest hits, strobe lights flashing, and mirror balls reflecting the dancers, discos were the place to go in almost every city across the United

States. But getting in usually required the right look, and dancers wanted to wear materials that picked up the light from the disco balls.

In the 1977 film *Saturday Night Fever*, John Travolta exemplified the look for men: a three-piece white leisure suit paired with a shiny black shirt that was open at the chest. Men often accessorized their outfits with necklaces and medallions, while women were dressed in everything from hot pants (very short shorts made in velvet and silk) and micro-miniskirts to tight spandex pants, glittery tops, and luminescent gowns. Platform shoes were a favorite with both men and women.

Saturday Night Fever made John Travolta a fashion icon, and his white suit and chest-baring black shirt became *the* fashion staple for men in the late 1970s.

GLAM ROCK

Glam rock was more of a fashion statement than a style of rock music. Male musicians wore makeup, including eye shadow, eyeliner, and lipstick. They also cross-dressed and wore extreme platform shoes. Their appearance often shocked or offended the more conservative establishment. Wearing make-up was something men didn't do. David Bowie, a British rock star, had androgynous looks that lent credence to his various personas. As his alter-ego Ziggy Stardust, Bowie wore skintight catsuits and dyed his spiked hair red. Elton John, a flamboyant British musician, wore oversized glittery glasses. American musician Alice Cooper used false eyelashes, garish make-up, and wore women's clothes. Fans of glam rock followed the fashion leadership of their musical idols.

PUNK

Another type of music that had a major influence on fashion in the late 1970s was punk. Punk rock had an abrasive attitude, directly confronting the establishment. Americans Patti Smith and the Ramones and the British Sex Pistols were among the best-known punk rockers. The Sex Pistols, with their notoriously bad-mannered lead singer Johnny Rotten and infamous bass player Sid Vicious, exemplified the punk-rock lifestyle.

Punk fashion included ripped T-shirts, combat boots, heavy chains, and safety pins, not only on clothes, but also as ornaments pierced through lips and cheeks. Tattoos were common, as were black, straight-legged, or drainpipe pants and leather jackets. Women wore fishnet stockings paired with heavy Doc Martens boots. Their hair was spiked or cut asymmetrically. Punks went for an eclectic DIY look, going to secondhand stores, army-navy supply stores, and sex shops for their clothes. One shop, called "Sex," was owned by Malcolm McLaren, the

Vivienne Westwood (*bottom, left*) her partner, Malcolm McLaren (*bottom, right*) with three models in their London shop, in 1985.

manager of the Sex Pistols, and his partner, self-taught fashion designer Vivienne Westwood.

Westwood was known for her punk outfits, which featured pornographic imagery and shoes with extremely high heels. When Westwood realized that her fashions were influencing other designers, including Parisian Claude Montana's ready-to-wear line, she decided to seriously pursue a career in fashion. Westwood went on to design provocative collections that included underwear as outerwear, minicrinis (which were short skirts with hoops), and corsets, which she helped revive. Westwood is considered one of the most innovative designers of the 1990s. She designed the wedding gown worn by Carrie Bradshaw (played by Sarah Jessica Parker) in the 2008 movie *Sex and the City*. Punk fashion, as well as Vivienne Westwood's designer collections, has continued into the twenty-first century.

THE MOTOWN LOOK

Motown Records, founded by Berry Gordy in 1959, had a huge number of well-known performers, including Smokey Robinson, Stevie Wonder, The Temptations, and The Supremes, all of whom had enormous crossover appeal. In the 1960s, the conservative hairstyles and stylish clothes of The Supremes were copied by their admirers. A decade later, the Jackson 5, with its Afro hairstyles, was one of the top groups. Teenage fans from all over the country cut their hair in the same Afro hairstyles, and started wearing Jackson 5–inspired bell-bottomed jeans and fringe vests.

THE REGGAE LOOK

Dreadlocks, sometimes called dreads, are matted coils of hair often worn by followers of the Rastafarian religious movement that began in Jamaica. Reggae musicians introduced this hairstyle to American culture in the late 1970s. At the time, the best-known reggae musicians were Bob Marley and the Wailers. Dreadlocks have remained popular not only with Rastafarians, but have also been adopted by surfers and skateboarders.

1970S FASHION, FILM, AND TELEVISION

Movies have always played a role in influencing fashion, but this seemed especially true in the 1970s. At the beginning of the decade, *Love Story* was released, and star Ali MacGraw's sophisticated, preppy look—camel coat, black tights, and knit hat and scarf—was copied by millions of women.

T-SHIRTS

Whether worn as underwear under uniforms for the armed forces or as the latest must-have trend in fashion, the T-shirt has changed very little in its basic design since it was first mass-produced in the mid–nineteenth century. In the 1930s, colleges and universities used T-shirts printed with school logos as sports uniforms. After World War II, the shirts were worn for physical labor or for sports. When Marlon Brando wore one in his role of the earthy, sexy, working-class Stanley Kowalski in *A Streetcar Named Desire* in 1951, the T-shirt achieved a type of glamour. Like jeans, the T-shirt soon became popular with rebels and nonconformists, whether they were beatniks or hippies.

T-shirts became a means of expression because it was easy to print images and messages on them. "Make Love Not War" was one of the most popular sayings imprinted on shirts worn by anti-war activists during the war in Vietnam. Tie-dyed T-shirts were often worn by hippies, and they also became a symbol of Deadheads—fans of the Grateful Dead.

In the 1980s, black T-shirts became trendy and T-shirts with designer logos became status symbols. Designer Michael Kors, a former judge on the TV show *Project Runway*, has made the T-shirt his everyday uniform as well as his attire for the show. Today, T-shirts are used to promote everything from restaurants to sports teams to bands, serving as advertising and a means of self-expression.

The 1973 film adaptation of *The Great Gatsby* brought jazz-age 1920s clothes back into style with baggy trousers and bow ties for men and cloche hats and low-waisted skirts for women. The Gatsby look meant that black lashes and smudged eye shadow were also back in vogue.

In 1977, Woody Allen's *Annie Hall* debuted. Diane Keaton, who played Annie Hall, dressed in many of her own clothes, with their Ralph Lauren labels. She wore men's hats, a vest and a tie, and combined an oversized tweed jacket with a feminine shirt. The Annie Hall look took off, and the distinction between men's and women's clothing styles blurred further as women started buying clothes in the menswear departments.

"Blaxploitation" films were controversial for their portrayal of black men as gangsters and drug users, but influential in terms of fashion. The clothing worn in the films both influenced and reflected what people were wearing on the street. *Shaft* (1971), with Richard Roundtree in the starring role as a private detective, popularized the "radical chic" style of young urban black men. The look included boots with stacked heels, tight pants that were not jeans, three-quarter-length leather jackets, and black turtlenecks. Tamara Dobson played a sexy drug agent in *Cleopatra Jones* (1973). Her wardrobe included stylish 1970s fashions ranging from platform shoes to flowing skirts and wide-legged pants.

The TV series *Charlie's Angels* (1976–1981) brought sex appeal into American homes with three female private detectives. The original Angels, played by actresses Kate Jackson, Jaclyn Smith, and Farrah Fawcett-Majors, often went braless on the show, turning what had been a political statement in the early days of women's liberation into mainstream pop culture. Farrah Fawcett-Majors's layered hair with its flowing curls became one of the most popular hairstyles for women, even though hot rollers and curling irons were required to maintain the look.

DRESS FOR SUCCESS

Many young people didn't have a clue about what to wear to make it in the corporate world, and if they wanted a job, appearance mattered. In a 1976 article entitled "Good-bye, Love Beads. Hello, Watch Chain," *Forbes*, a leading business magazine, wrote "a young guy can't go looking for a job in jeans and a Levi jacket and relate to the guy sitting across the desk from him." Young women entering the workplace also needed advice on what to wear. As a result of the women's movement, more women wanted middle and upper-management positions in the corporate world as well as in the professions. They needed to know how to dress the part.

John Molloy, a business writer and image consultant, wrote two books on fashion in the workplace: *Dress for Success* (1975) and *The Women's Dress for Success Book* (1977). Molloy wrote that traditional, conservative suits were authority symbols and recommended that shirts should be made of cotton or a cotton-polyester blend.

In *The Women's Dress for Success Book*, Molloy stated that women would do best on the job "if their uniform consists of a conservative skirted suit, preferably blue, with light colored blouse, preferably white. And they must wear plain pumps, never boots." Molloy allowed some leeway if women worked in offices where men did not wear suits, or if they worked in high-fashion industries, such as media, art, and fashion.

Career clothing became a viable market, and designers such as Liz Claiborne, Jones of New York, and Evan Picone began catering to career women. Stores like Ann Taylor and Brooks Brothers expanded their women's departments. Liz Claiborne said, "I envision my clothes for working women, although that's not always the case. Actually, they're for active, young-minded women who want to put themselves together for under $150."

THE CHANGING ROLE OF DESIGNERS AND "FASHION"

Fashion critic Kennedy Fraser remembers the 1970s as a unique time in women's fashion, writing, "By chance, I took over the Feminine Fashions column of the *New Yorker* (in 1970) at the very moment that feminine fashions ceased to count. . . . After that, there was no longer any unabashedly accepted, universal fashion authority . . . " While a single designer could change the "look," as Dior did in the 1940s and 1950s, and Courrèges and Mary Quant did in the 1960s, by the 1970s, change in fashion became more gradual as other factors came into play.

The most important of these was fashion branding. Branding had always been a means of identification of specific items, from Levi jeans with its back pocket label to Louis Vuitton bags with their repeated "LV" logos. But in the 1970s, branding began to play an even more important role in the fashion world as the image and marketing of a fashion line became more critical than the actual design of the clothes. For successful branding, the image needs to be meaningful and to represent a lifestyle that entices the buyers. Fashion marketers became expert at branding and, by 2004, a study showed that children as young as five years old were familiar with branded sportswear. It also showed that, as they got older, they recognized that brands could be used as status symbols and as a way to belong to a certain group. Branding also allows designers to license their name to other products, from perfume to sunglasses to home furnishings.

Several fashion designers who exemplified the importance of branding made their name by using it in the 1970s. Halston, the designer of Jackie Kennedy's pillbox hat in the 1960s, became one of the leaders of fashion minimalism—the idea that less is more—a major trend of the 1970s. Halston was known for using Ultrasuede, an artificial fiber that looks

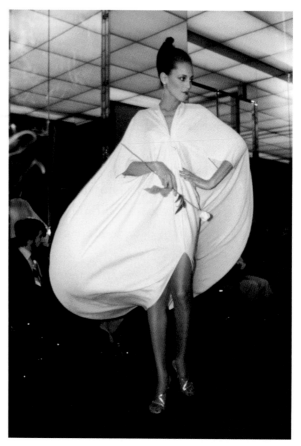

Halston was one of the premier designers of the 1970s. Known for Ultrasuede, he also designed whimsical evening wear, such as this puffed dress that filled with air like a parachute when the woman wearing it moved.

like suede but can be washed. He created soft trousers and tunics for day and night, and sweater sets in cashmere, argyle, and matte jersey. He designed disco fashion as well.

Calvin Klein, another fashion minimalist, established his own company in the late 1960s. By the mid–1970s he was known for his casual yet elegant separates. Klein often said, "I make clothes people like to wear," and his success over the years proves his statement. Klein has also superbly marketed his jeans and underwear lines.

Ralph Lauren, with his Polo Fashions, began as a menswear tie designer. Lauren reinterpreted Ivy League classics and clothes associated with English gentlemen. He added cowboy and safari touches and created a highly successful women's line. He said, "I'm not just selling clothes. I'm offering a world, a philosophy of life," and his advertisements, which used little or no ad copy, reinforced this idea.

Diane von Fürstenberg introduced the wrap dress, a V-neck dress that wrapped around the body and was secured by a sash. It could be worn in an office or out for the evening. The style was such a hit with American women—who bought over five million V-neck dresses in the 1970s—that von Fürstenberg landed on the cover of *Newsweek* magazine in 1976.

DECADE IN REVIEW

The 1970s were a time of transition in American society and fashion. Many of the activities and causes from the 1960s, including women's rights, civil rights, gay rights, and environmental activism, achieved greater acceptance. But there was also a sense of despair during the 1970s because of, among other events, rampant inflation, gas shortages and the Watergate scandal, which led to the resignation of President Nixon.

"Fashion," as such, was not in fashion, as demonstrated by the rejection of the midi-skirt at the beginning of the decade. The 1970s are often now seen as a time of bad taste, with hot pants and leisure suits as prime examples. The fitness boom and the desire to climb the corporate ladder provided new clothing niches, and music, as always, influenced fashion trends from punk to disco to glam rock.

Branding helped usher in a new group of designers, a new philosophy of clothing, and became possibly the most important fashion trend in the last quarter of the twentieth century and beyond.

FOUR

1980s:
The Age of Consumerism

AMERICANS REDISCOVERED THEIR SENSE OF optimism in the 1980s. President Ronald Reagan used the slogan "It's morning again in America" for his successful reelection campaign in 1984, reminding voters that with him as president the economy was booming and they could look to the future with confidence.

There was no longer any such thing as one prevailing fashion. What was considered fashionable depended more than ever on the "group" or subset someone belonged to. The specific style of dress of the group was a means of identification for members.

Yuppies, for example, wore preppy clothes. The Yuppies— young urban professionals—were men and women striving for upward mobility, and its corresponding high income and power. *Newsweek* published a cartoon by *Doonesbury* creator Gary Trudeau of Yuppies on its cover and called 1984, "The Year of the Yuppie."

For the Yuppies, fashion was a status symbol—no matter what the cost. In fact, during the Reagan years of the 1980s, showing off well-known labels, whether they were a designer's name or the logo of a casual brand, was crucial. With a booming economy and the desire for conspicuous consumption, spending on luxury goods became widespread.

In the White House, Nancy Reagan, the most fashion-conscious first lady since Jackie Kennedy, was wearing well-known American designers, including Adolfo, James Galanos, Oscar de la Renta, Carolina Herrera, and Bill Blass. Rich socialites went for Christian Lacroix, who made the "pouf" or "bubble" cocktail dress with frills galore, as well as other luxurious clothes. Another favorite was Karl Lagerfeld, who modernized the Chanel look. Lagerfeld introduced materials, such as tweed and leather, to the line and gave several Chanel classics a new look and an easier fit. Italian Giorgio Armani, who designed sleek two-piece suits for Richard Gere in the film *American Gigolo* (1980), set trends with both men's and women's styles.

Nothing personified the 1980s like the so-called Yuppies, who were branded as much by their "Dress for Success" clothes as by their economic aspirations.

Both Yuppie males and successful older men wore brightly colored ties, often yellow or red, suspenders, and expensive designer label suits. Women's dress for success from the late 1970s morphed into power dressing, which was typified by broad-shouldered, heavily padded jackets with tight, slim skirts. The exaggerated shoulders, which were advertised as "the menswear look," may have been based on football players' uniforms. They provided an outward look of confidence. The films *Wall Street* (1987) and *Working Girl* (1988) were influenced by what people working on Wall Street wore and showed Yuppie stockbrokers in elegant double-breasted Italian suits, as well as New York working women wearing sneakers with their power suits as they walked down busy city streets to their offices. This trend started during the 1980 transit strike in New York City, when women needed comfortable footwear to get to work. Wearing sneakers or running shoes on the way to and from work and high heels while at the office became an accepted practice.

Designer Donna Karan offered women an alternative to power suits with her seven easy pieces: a bodysuit, pants, a skirt, a blazer, a blouse, a coat, and a piece for evening wear. With black tights and accessories, Karan's pieces provided interchangeable outfits that could easily go from the office to evening social occasions.

For casual wear, the "preppy" look was in. *The Official Preppy Handbook*, edited by Lisa Birnbach and published in 1980, was meant as a satire, but was taken seriously by some Yuppies. The guidelines called for the same classic conservative clothes popular in the 1950s: button-down oxford shirts, crew-neck sweaters, polo shirts, khaki pants or skirts, and loafers or boat shoes. Shetland and Fair Isle sweaters, madras prints, and tartan plaids were also part of the look. The preppy style called for a layered look, with one or more polo shirts under an oxford shirt, and a sweater tied over the shoulders.

The most important thing was to be sure that clothes had the "right" labels and came from the "right" stores. The top logo was the Lacoste alligator logo, but L. L. Bean, Polo Ralph Lauren, and J. Crew were also very popular. This casual look was reminiscent of the decades when the dominant class in the United States was "white Anglo-Saxon Protestant" (or WASP). This led to a very different look than the ethnic styles that were worn by hippies in the 1960s and 1970s.

Buying clothes for the casual look was easy because malls, which had first appeared in the 1950s, were everywhere by the 1980s. The 1983 film *Valley Girl* highlighted the mall culture as a place to socialize as well as shop. Valley girls had their own look: blond or bleached-blond hair, leggings, skirts with lace, and plastic jelly shoes. They also had their own way of speaking, using the words "like" and "totally" in just about every sentence. Specialized retail stores with affordable yet fashionable clothes could be found in almost every mall. Some of the best known were the Gap, United Colors of Benetton, Ann Taylor, Banana Republic, and The Limited.

JAPANESE DESIGNERS

Avant-garde Japanese designers attracted a lot of attention in the 1980s. Kenzo Takada and Issey Miyake had begun showing in Paris in the 1970s. Kenzo's clothes blended eastern and western influences, while Issey Miyake was known for his new and experimental materials. In the 1980s, Rei Kawakubo and her business, Comme des Garçons, came to Paris, as did Japanese designer Yohji Yamamoto. Kawakubo and Yamamoto started the deconstructionist trend in fashion, which emphasized the shape and construction of a garment as opposed to the person wearing it. Their clothes were often rectangular and androgynous. The frayed seams and open edges they used would influence clothing collections in future years.

EXERCISE BECOMES FITNESS

Aerobics became *the* fitness obsession during the 1980s. Academy Award–winning actress Jane Fonda released the first of her many aerobic exercise videos in 1982. Workout apparel, with leg warmers as the must-have accessory, became even more fashionable than it had been in the 1970s. Leggings were available in every color and pattern, and young women paired them with long pullover sweaters. Girls copied Jennifer Beals's outfits in *Flashdance* (1983) and dangled sweatshirts off one shoulder. They paired the look with matching leg warmers and headbands, tank tops, and tight-fitting jeans. At that time, too, fashionistas went for the Tunisian-born designer Azzedine Alaia's clinging, body-conscious clothing.

For outdoor wear, manufacturers took advantage of Gore-Tex and Thinsulate, innovative new fabrics that could be used for wind resistance and waterproofing

In 1982, Reebok introduced a soft leather athletic shoe specifically for women. In 1985, Nike launched the first Air Jordan basketball shoes, endorsed by Chicago Bulls rookie Michael Jordan. Air Jordans were so popular and expensive that "shoe jackings," in which people were robbed for their shoes, occurred primarily in poor neighborhoods during the mid– and late 1980s.

Nike's 1988 advertising campaign slogan, "Just Do It," was chosen by *Ad Age* magazine as one of the top two taglines of the twentieth century. Keeping fit had become a persuasive idea, and running shoes were now a fashion statement!

1980S TELEVISION CREATES FASHION TRENDS

With few exceptions, television reflected what Americans were wearing during the 1950s, 1960s, and 1970s. In the 1980s, television helped to fashion new styles and reintroduce old ones. *Magnum P.I.* (1980–1988), a series about a private eye in Hawaii, was one of the most popular TV shows of the decade. Many men who watched not only admired star Tom Selleck's bushy mustache and Hawaiian shirts, but also found them worth imitating. *The A Team* (1983–1987) made gold chains and Mohawk hairstyles popular, while *The Cosby Show* (1984–1992) gave a boost to bright-patterned sweaters like those worn by Bill Cosby and the crown hair style of Malcom-Jamal Warner.

There were programs specifically about fashion, such as CNN's *Style with Elsa Klensch*, which began in 1980 and included classic fashions and designers as well as trend-setting styles. In the late 1980s, MTV created *House of Style* hosted by fashion supermodel Cindy Crawford. The show featured fashion that appealed to teens and young adults. Shopping channels debuted, beginning with QVC (Quality, Value, and Convenience) in 1986. However, the greatest impact on American style was made by two television series, *Miami Vice* and *Dynasty*, and a new network, MTV.

MIAMI VICE (1984–1990)

Miami Vice was set in South Beach, Miami, and centered on two vice cops. South Beach's art deco architecture gave the series its unique look, with pastel and fluorescent colors used for both the sets and costumes. Detective James Crockett, played by Don Johnson, wore casual trousers and T-shirts in pastel shades under rumpled Italian linen jackets, often with the sleeves pushed up. His unconstructed blazers, pleated pants, and loafers without socks became a fashionable style in menswear. Johnson also popularized the unshaven look and the Ray-Ban Wayfarer sunglasses that were also worn by Tom Cruise in the films *Risky Business* (1983) and *Top Gun* (1986).

Detective Ricardo Tubbs, played by Philip Michael Thomas, wore silk shirts with slender neckties, double-breasted suits, and a diamond stud in his ear. The series brought Italian men's fashion to the American viewing public's attention: the uncon-

LADY DIANA AS A FASHION ICON

Diana Spencer married Prince Charles of the United Kingdom on July 29, 1981, in what seemed to be a fairytale story come to life. Her wedding dress, with its 25-foot train designed by Elizabeth and David Emanuel, was seen by more than one billion people when the ceremony was broadcast worldwide. Known as a "meringue dress" because of its huge puffball sleeves and full skirt, Diana's wedding dress influenced bridal style in the 1980s.

From the moment Diana became engaged, everything she wore was scrutinized and copied. Her short haircut with its fluffy layers became very popular, as did the sling-back shoes she often wore. With the help of British designer Catherine Walker, Princess Diana created a modern version of the traditional look required for her role as a member of the royal family. After her divorce in 1996, Diana opted for a more sophisticated international look with clothes designed by Dior, Lacroix, and Chanel as well as Italian designers Versace and Valentino. She died in a car accident in 1997.

After her divorce in 1996, Princess Diana turned to the sophisticated styles of Christian Lacroix. His elaborate costumes, such as this embroidered black jacket and balloon dress, were a hit with other wealthy socialites, as well.

structed or floppy suit was an Italian staple and wearing a T-shirt instead of a collared shirt under a jacket was a look from Italian designer Gianni Versace. In 1985, the Council for the Fashion Designers of American gave awards to *Miami Vice* and Ray-Ban for their contributions to fashion.

DYNASTY (1981–1989)

Dynasty was an evening soap opera that aired on ABC in the 1980s. The two female leads, Krystle and Alexis, played by Linda Evans and Joan Collins, represented good and evil. One of the draws of the series for the viewing audience was getting a peek at the fashions and lifestyles of the rich and stylish women on the show.

Krystle wore subtle pastels or white. Her soft clothes included long-sleeved silk blouses with broad, padded shoulders. The broad shoulders for both day and evening wear made Krystle's silhouette look like an inverted triangle—the dominant look of successful women in the 1980s. Krystle's long blond hair was occasionally worn in an upsweep, which got bigger from season to season. Big hair was another major trend of the 1980s. Alexis's trademarks were her hats—sometimes with a veil, other times with a large brim. She would also wear suits that ranged in color from bright hues to black and white. Both women wore extravagant jewelry for nighttime events.

The show's costume designer, Nolan Miller, not only chose designer clothing for the stars, but designed some himself. His fashions became such a hit that when "The Dynasty Collection" was presented at Bloomingdale's in New York City, more than 20,000 shoppers showed up for the launch of the line.

MTV

On August 1, 1981, a new cable channel debuted, with rock-and-roll music videos airing round-the-clock. MTV targeted

teenagers and twenty-somethings. This new youth generation—people born from 1965 to 1976, known as Generation X
or Gen Xers—was the offspring of the baby-boom generation.
MTV showed music videos that influenced every aspect of
American culture, from advertising to fashion. In a way, MTV
became an ongoing fashion show as fans watched and copied
what their favorite performers wore.

Cyndi Lauper, with her punk hairdo—dyed bright red
and shaved on one side—and outrageous costumes, came to
stardom on MTV with her "Girls Just Want to Have Fun"
video. Another MTV star was Duran Duran, a British pop
group whose trend-setting look, featuring skinny pants and
ties and lavish use of eyeliner, was as big a part of the group's
success as their music. Michael Jackson's single sequined glove
with matching socks could be seen in the videos for his album
Thriller. The look was copied by his fans, as was his many-
zipped red leather jacket.

RAP AND HIP-HOP

Rap, or speaking in rhyme to music (hip-hop), started in the late
1970s at parties in the Bronx, New York. It is based on the Jamai-
can reggae sound and the African oral tradition of toasting.

It wasn't until 1984, when Run–D.M.C. had their first
rap single played on MTV, that hip-hop started to become
mainstream. Run–D.M.C. performed in leather pants, leather
jackets, unlaced Adidas sneakers, and fedora hats. They even
had a hit song called "My Adidas," but made sure to include in
the lyrics that their Adidas sneakers only brought good news.
The reason: while wearing sneakers without laces was a fashion
statement, it was also a very street thing to do, especially for
young men who had just been in jail or wanted to look like they
may have been in jail. Convicts aren't allowed to have shoelaces
for fear they might hang themselves or hurt someone else.

MADONNA AS A FASHION ICON

Bursting on the scene with her first album in 1982, Madonna launched trends, from teased blonde hair with black roots to black lace gloves, stiletto heels, cross-shaped earrings, fluorescent rubber bracelets, and heavy make-up. With each album and video, Madonna created a new persona, going from a bridal gown and white lace corsets for "Like a Virgin," to copying Marilyn Monroe from the film *Gentlemen Prefer Blondes* for her video "Material Girl."

Her ever-evolving look has included androgynous, punk, S&M (sadomasochism), western, and military styles, among others. In 1990, she wore Jean-Paul Gaultier's pink corset with a cone bra for her Blonde Ambition World Tour and wore his neo-punk fashions for her 2001 Drowned World Tour.

Madonna promoted haute couture and appeared in ads for mainstream fashion stores like the Gap. Her influence has changed the way hundreds of thousands of women have dressed from the 1980s to the present day. Whether she is wearing underwear as outerwear or baring her navel as she performs, Madonna is an icon of modern fashion.

In the 1980s the pop singer Madonna seemed to be known at least as well for her bold fashion statements as for her music. Her cone bras and flashy outfits were copied by teen girls everywhere.

Rap style also included black baggy clothes, large chain necklaces, rings, oversized T-shirts, large sunglasses, and Kangol-brand hats. Some rap and hip-hop fans and performers shaved words into their hair or wore what is called the "fade" haircut, which was high on top and shaved close on the side. Others wore a sideways baseball cap.

PUNK AND GOTH: REVIVALS AND INTROS

The punk look continued and by the early 1980s, the most easily recognizable punk hairstyle, the Mohawk, also called the Mohican, came into fashion. Some punks transitioned into Goths, inspired in part by Goth music and the Goth style of dressing. Cintra Wilson, in a *New York Times* article describing her life in late 1980s San Francisco wrote, "Goth was a fashion response to doing infrequent laundry and never seeing the sun." Goth was typified by black clothing and pale complexions.

To fashion historians, Goth also incorporated Gothic literature and film, including vampire films, "medieval religious iconography, and Victorian mourning costumes." Tattoos of crosses and mystical symbols were popular among both male and female Goths. Goths could wear anything from black jeans and a T-shirt to more elaborate costumes with mourning veils, corsets, fishnet stockings, and Doc Martens or Victorian-style lace-up boots. Goth fashion has become an enduring subculture.

DECADE IN REVIEW

With President Ronald Reagan in the White House for the majority of the 1980s and the economy booming, conspicuous consumption, including spending money on expensive, sophisticated, and glamorous clothes, was a sign of the times. On TV shows such as *Dynasty* and *Miami Vice* new fashions were on display, and the public was eager to try them. "Fashion is

The 1980s Goth style was epitomized by heavy Egyptian-style eyeliner, spiked dyed-black hair with long, often asymmetrical bangs, and black leather, lace, or velvet clothing.

SKATEBOARDING

By the 1980s, skateboarding had become very popular, as had the skater look, even with people who couldn't stay on a board. A T-shirt, baggy cargo pants, and a hoodie, plus wide sneakers with fat laces were all that was needed to look like someone who could swoop up and down a ramp while doing stunts on a tiny board. Popular brands that catered to skateboarders included Airwalk, Vans, and Vision. By the 1990s, mainstream shoe and clothing companies entered the market as well.

change," said designer Karl Lagerfeld. "I'm bored by designers who have one style and never want to move from that, because the interesting thing about fashion is that it reflects, over a very short period, the spirit of the moment."

As baby boomers moved into executive positions, they went for power clothing at work and for casual wear at home. These fashions were similar to what they had worn in their youth—an updated version of the preppy styles of the 1950s, but this time with designer labels. The ethnic clothing from the previous decades was still around, but for the Gen Xers, music, and especially what they saw on MTV, was a primary influence for fashion trends. Hip-hop, rap, punk, and Goth all added their own distinctive styles to the 1980s.

1990s:
The Information Age

IN THE 1990S, THE INTERNET CAME OF AGE and profoundly changed the way people communicated, worked, shopped, and dressed. For those working in the computer industry—including entrepreneurs whose companies had profits in the billions—casual clothing was the way to dress. Chinos, jeans, sneakers, and T-shirts were the new norm for many businesses, and wearing business attire was only necessary at conservative companies such as banks and investment firms. Casual Fridays became common and, by 1998, four out of five workers were allowed to dress down at least one day a week in what was called "business casual." The definition of business casual depended on the company—at some companies, jeans, spandex, leggings, sneakers, and sandals were not allowed, while at other offices, employees could wear almost anything they wanted.

Abercrombie & Fitch became a trendsetter for teens, competing with J. Crew, American Eagle, and the Gap. In fact, casual, inexpensive clothing became a status symbol when actor Sharon Stone appeared at the 1996 Oscars wearing a black Gap turtleneck with a Valentino skirt. She was one of

In the 1990s, dressing down became the new form of office attire. If Steve Jobs, visionary co-founder of Apple, could wear jeans to work, why not the rest of us, seemed to be the ethos.

the earliest influences in combining "high and low" fashion, pairing pieces from haute couture designers with mainstream ready-to-wear labels.

INFLUENCE OF MUSIC

"As the lines between fashion and rock and roll continue to blur, it's anyone's guess who's influencing whom these days," a reporter for the fashion newspaper *Women's Wear Daily* wrote in the late–1990s. "Are designers looking to rock for inspiration, or is the music biz borrowing from the runways?" In fact, music, as always, was a major influence on what young people wore. As street fashion became more popular, designers took note and worked it into their own collections. Grunge was a prime example. American designers Marc Jacobs and Anna Sui, and European designers Dolce & Gabbana and Gianni Versace all added elements of grunge to their collections in the 1990s.

GRUNGE

Grunge originated in Seattle in the early 1990s, with Nirvana and Pearl Jam as two of the best-known bands. The music

One of the top American designers of the 1990s was Anna Sui, who mixed high fashion with grunge.

appealed to a sense of alienation felt by many teenagers. The alternative rock music had a strong beat, with electric guitars driving the sound. Fans would often gather in mosh pits, an area typically in front of the stage, where they would jump around, push, and slam into each other.

The clothing style was rumpled, disheveled, and casual, and the clothes themselves were often ripped and torn. Many of the garments were bought at thrift and second-hand shops. Men wore T-shirts and long-sleeved flannel shirts tied around their waists. Their pants could be baggy jeans, corduroys, or cargo pants, worn low so that their boxer shorts were visible. Footwear was Doc Martens, vintage Converse, or Vans sneakers, which are cloth sneakers with no laces and thick rubber soles that come in many different colors and patterned designs. Hoodies and oversized sweaters were also popular.

Courtney Love, the lead singer and guitarist for Hole, was the inspiration for female fans. She wore baby-doll dresses, ripped fishnet stockings, Mary Jane shoes, and smeared makeup.

RAP AND HIP-HOP

In 1998, rap outsold country music, which had previously been the top-selling music format in America. Though rap and hip-hop had started in black and Latino urban neighborhoods, by this time white listeners bought more than 70 percent of hip-hop albums. Like grunge followers, rappers wore baggy pants so low on the hip that the tops of their designer boxers were displayed. Classic preppy lines, such as Tommy Hilfiger, Polo Ralph Lauren, Calvin Klein, and Nautica were the favorite brands of artists and fans because those labels represented style. When rapper Snoop Doggy Dogg wore an oversized Tommy Hilfiger rugby shirt on *Saturday Night Live* in 1994, Hilfiger sales boomed overnight. Hilfiger changed the direction of his line and became a brand linked with rap. (Years later, Hilfiger

Hip-hop influenced male fashion in the 1990s in a big way. Men took to wearing baggy, low-waisted jeans with huge shirts and big boots.

returned to its traditional preppy style.) A number of hip-hop artists moved onto high-end labels including Dolce & Gabbana, Versace, Prada, and Gucci, to create an image of privilege and status.

Female rapper Lil' Kim referenced Dolce & Gabbana in her 1996 song "Drugs" from her album *Hardcore* with the line, "Call us the Gabbana girls." Lil' Kim became known for her outrageous outfits, and for pushing fashion boundaries—especially after having exposed her left breast (with the nipple covered by a purple pastie) at the MTV Video Music Awards. Several months before at the VH1/Vogue Fashion Awards in 1999 she said, "When it comes to fashion, there's no such thing as going too far."

In the 1990s, FUBU (For Us By Us) entered the hip-hop market. Several rappers launched their own clothing brands as well. Phat Farm, started by Russell Simmons, the cofounder of Def Jam Records, and Sean John, developed by Sean "P. Diddy" Combs, were just two of them.

A new phrase became popular in the 1990s—bling-bling. In 1999, Baby Gangsta's (B.G.) song "Bling-Bling" made the term, which had originally referred to outrageous jewelry and ornaments such as the jewel-encrusted tooth caps worn by some hip-hop artists, more widespread. In time, bling came to mean any type of flashy, expensive possessions, from cars to clothes to gadgets.

TEEN POP

Just as Madonna was imitated by young women in the 1980s, a number of young female singers and boy bands became fashion leaders for teenagers and young people in the mid– and late 1990s. Often, these singers and bands were promoted for their image as well as for their music.

In 1994, marketers created the Spice Girls, a pop group of five young British women, meant to appeal to preteens. Each of the girls was known by a nickname—Scary, Baby, Ginger, Sporty, and Posh—based on her image. Scary had untamed curly hair, a pierced tongue, and wore tight slacks and revealing bras. Baby Spice represented another version of femininity, with her pigtails and baby doll dresses. Ginger Spice had red hair and wore tight, bright clothing as well as corsets, garters, and stockings, while Sporty Spice dressed in workout suits and exercise bras with her hair in a ponytail. Posh Spice was known for her stylish clothes and high heels. The Spice Girls advocated "Girl Power." They showed a V for Victory sign with their fingers to indicate self-reliance, and to let adolescent girls know that almost any style of dressing was possible and legitimate.

Christina Aguilera, Britney Spears, Justin Timberlake, and JC Chasez were Mouseketeers on the last few seasons of *The All-New Mickey Mouse Club* (1989–1994), a new version of the show that was popular in the 1950s. When the program went off the air, Timberlake and Chasez became part of *NSYNC along with Chris Kirkpatrick, Joey Fatone, and Lance Bass. The group had a number of hits in the late 1990s. Like the Spice Girls, each member of the group had a role to play. Boy bands such as *NSYNC and the Backstreet Boys usually included a rebel, a jock, the star, the sensitive soul, and the bad boy. The dress was relatively clean-cut— T-shirts, oversized jeans, and leather jackets.

Britney Spears toured with *NSYNC as an opening act. The music video for her first single ". . . Baby One More Time" aired on MTV in 1998. In the video, she wears a schoolgirl uniform with a miniskirt, which led to the popularity of box-pleated cheerleader skirts and mini-versions of Catholic schoolgirl skirts among young women. Spears became a superstar, and her attire in many of her videos helped promote the trends for the thong and belly shirts.

Like Britney, Christina Aguilera went on to a singing career. Getting rid of her teeny-bopper image, Aguilera had her nickname—Xtina— tattooed on the back of her neck and got several body piercings. She also developed a new raunchy persona for her album, "Stripped." By the 2000s, she had traded that look and attitude for a more glamorous one, becoming the face of Versace in their advertisements, one of the main fashion influences for teenagers. She also developed her own fragrance line.

Jennifer Lopez's first national television appearance was on the comedy sketch program *In Living Color*, as a "Fly Girl," or dancer. Lopez, who is also called JLo, became well-known when she starred in the 1998 film *Selena*, about the Mexican American singer of that name. A year later, JLo released her first record album; she has been releasing songs and making movies ever since. When Lopez gained celebrity status, fans imitated her clothing choices. Fans of pop singers, boy bands, and rappers tried to copy what they saw their idols wearing on TV and in videos. However, some fashion had gone too far for parents and principals. Public schools imposed strict dress codes, banning spaghetti-strap tank tops, micro-miniskirts, midriff-baring outfits, and pants that revealed underwear.

REVIVAL OF GOTH

In the 1990s, the Goth trend resurfaced, in part because of the Internet, which made it possible for Goths around the world to communicate. At the same time, the band Marilyn Manson adopted Goth makeup with its black hair, white faces, black eyeliner, black lipstick, and black nail polish.

As Goth fashion became more popular, it divided itself into various categories: Industrial Goth was characterized by goggles, black trousers or military cargo pants, and military accessories for men and waist-cinching corsets for women. Cyber Goths

The Goth trend revived in the 1990s, with the band Marilyn Manson embracing the black makeup and white, white skin that identified the subgroup.

wore black clothing with huge platform boots, synthetic metallic fibers, and bleached hair. Gothabilly incorporated 1950s fashion, and Gothic Lolita mixed Japanese influences to create an innocent look with sensuality and rebellion. Goth fashion has even found its way onto one of America's favorite TV series. NCIS, which began in 2003, features forensic specialist Abby Sciuto wearing Goth clothing under her white lab coat.

RAVERS

Raves, parties held at underground clubs, were the place to be for young people who wanted to dance the night away. The dancing at raves was often accompanied by the use of drugs, especially Ecstasy. The raver look is one of few trends where dance, rather than music, was the inspiration for loose-fitting clothing, including T-shirts, baggy pants, and hoodies. Their clothing was often brightly colored and paired with glow-in-the-dark accessories, such as pacifiers and glow ropes.

CELEBRITY INFLUENCES FROM TV TO SUPERMODELS

Friends (1994–2004) was one of the most popular sitcoms of all time, and Jennifer Aniston's layered hairstyle, called "The Rachel" after the character she played, was copied by many of her fans. Aniston's character became such a fashion icon that a single episode would inspire tens of thousands of calls about where to find an article of clothing worn during the episode.

HBO's *Sex and the City* (1998–2004), based on the book of the same name by Candace Bushnell, was one of the most influential television shows in terms of fashion. Each of the four female characters had a distinct style. Kim Cattrall's Samantha tended to dress seductively while Kristin Davis as Charlotte wore preppy attire. Cynthia Nixon played Miranda, a lawyer whose outfits reflected the choices of a successful career woman. The show's main character, Carrie, played by Sarah Jessica Parker, became a fashion icon. Viewers imitated her eccentric styles, from showing bra straps to wearing fabric flowers. Carrie's wardrobe was a mix of designer clothes and finds from flea markets. Costume designer Patricia Field was responsible for the total look of the show. *Sex and the City* made Manolo Blahnik and Jimmy Choo stilettos, Fendi baguettes (bags), Prada, and Dolce & Gabbana, as well as nameplate necklaces, the must-have items and brands for hundreds of thousands of fans.

This relationship between television stars and fashion is fostered by the marketing of fashion brands and designers. The designers work with the shows' costumers and with stylists to get their apparel seen on specific shows. Trends are then set as viewers buy the clothes their idols wear.

Trends were also set by another type of celebrity in the 1990s—fashion models, who became superstars and "the biggest news in fashion." The year 1992 was the height of supermodel stardom. Models such as Cindy Crawford, Naomi Campbell, Linda Evangelista, Claudia Schiffer, and Christy Turlington became major celebrities. Their names were known by people far outside the fashion industry. These women were paid millions because they could "make consumers buy." They also served as role models with their toned bodies. Victoria's Secret, the largest American lingerie store, with its models Gisele Bundchen and Heidi Klum, reinforced this strong image as it brought sexy lingerie into the mainstream. Push-up bras, such as the Wonderbra, the UltraBra, and the Miracle Bra, enabled women to both create and show off cleavage. By the late 1990s, the ideal image went from buxom to an extremely thin, "heroin chic" appearance, as exemplified by supermodel Kate Moss.

BODY ART

While tattoos were once a sign of criminals, gang members, sailors, and bikers, they became more socially acceptable in the 1990s as rock stars, actors, models, and athletes exhibited all types of tattoos and body piercings. By wearing clothes that showed off their tattoos, these high-profile celebrities helped create a market for upscale, custom art tattoo studios. Belly button piercings led to the popularity of the midriff-baring "belly shirt."

However, parents of teenagers urged state legislators to take action against the tattooing or piercing of anyone under the age of eighteen without a parent present. By the mid–1990s, fifteen states had laws restricting or regulating the practice. Though the laws may have had little practical effect, they helped draw attention to the need to get a tattoo in a sterile environment from a reputable tattoo artist who follows safety practices.

DECADE IN REVIEW

The 1990s were a decade when people developed their own style by mixing top names with mass brands. It was also when business attire was largely replaced by casual clothes in many offices. Khakis, the symbol of casual dress because they could be worn almost any time and anywhere, were featured in a series of TV ads for the Gap, with khaki-clad dancers performing to a variety of music styles from swing to hip-hop. Music played a major role, with grunge, hip-hip, and teen pop idols influencing fashion styles.

Perhaps the most important influence on both fashion and pop culture in the 1990s was technology. With the arrival of the Internet, information, including the latest fashion styles and trends, could now be communicated in ways never before possible, which led to the emergence of a shared global culture.

SIX

2000s:
Fast Fashion

EVEN THOUGH AMERICANS WERE accustomed to the fast turnaround of trendy clothing styles sold at affordable stores such as Express and Target, Sweden's H&M changed the playing field even more. H&M opened its first U.S. store in 2000. By 2004 the clothing manufacturer could turn a design into a finished garment hanging on store racks in twenty days. Another chain, Spain's Zara, could do so in two weeks, though at higher prices. What this meant was that there were new looks at low prices almost constantly for anyone who wanted to be wearing the latest trend.

This was a major change from the twentieth century, when fashion companies would introduce new styles for spring, summer, autumn, winter, and perhaps an intermediate collection in between. A fast turnaround would be three months. Even today, no customer of luxury fashion would expect a weekly product change. Fast fashion has also introduced a discount designer collaboration in which well-known designers create

The discount chain H&M revolutionized ready-to-wear by its ability to quickly produce less expensive versions of high-fashion lines. Here, model Christine Lanvin models some of their wear.

special limited-edition collections for stores as diverse as Target, H&M, and Macy's. (The demand for Missoni's Target line was so great when it launched in September 2011 that users flooded the store's website, causing it to crash.) All of this is possible because of the advances of technology and the global supply network, where clothing companies outsource manufacturing to factories, mainly in Asia and Europe, that are able to produce low-cost products quickly and efficiently.

With the expansion of the Internet, the growing popularity of Facebook and YouTube, and websites that show the latest fashions and where to get them at the lowest cost possible, fashion has become anyone's game.

THE ECONOMY AND FASHION

Americans had dealt with minor economic slowdowns in 1987 and 2001, but the 2008 recession put an end to much of the spending on high-priced fashions that started in the Reagan years. Few people wanted to be seen shopping in high-end stores when hundreds of thousands of people were out of work. Some buyers would ask salespeople to put their purchases in plain bags rather than those advertising an expensive label.

With a slow economy, do-it-yourself fashion came to the forefront. Consumers cut down on their purchases or bought clothes in consignment shops. Vintage items and clothing came back into style.

VINTAGE

Vintage had always been around. Society women with vast collections of designer clothes would take them out every few years, taking pride in the superb tailoring and fabrics of the clothes they owned. Movie stars would often wear a vintage designer dress on the runway. But in the 2000s, vintage became a great way for fashionistas to make a great personal-style statement by wearing old designer or name-brand clothes. H&M jumped on the vintage bandwagon in 2006 by introducing a vintage corner in selected stores, where old garments can be bought but cannot be returned. Vintage stores exist everywhere, and flea markets, street fairs, and garage sales offer opportunities for buyers with a discerning eye to find fashions of the past. For some people, all it takes is going through their closets or attics.

Vintage takes a different turn with the steampunk trend. Steampunk is science fiction set in the Victorian age—an age of steam power, industrial invention, and petticoats. This fashion incorporates old-fashioned jewelry, such as pocket-watches, cameos, and driving goggles, along with Victorian-style vests and waistcoats for men, and bustle skirts and corsets for women. Modern gadgets, such as smart phones or mp3 players that have been given the appearance of Victorian-made products via decorative cases, as well as futuristic items described in Victorian literature, such as ray guns, are often used as accessories.

FASHION AND POPULAR CULTURE: SKIN IS "IN"

Pop singers made low-rise jeans, thongs, midriff-baring tops, and revealing décolletage popular, and TV series followed their lead. While high-level female executives in real life typically wear conservative clothes, on the medical series *House M.D.*, Dr. Lisa Cuddy, the hospital administrator, was frequently shown wearing very low-cut tops to work. Reality television's *Real Housewives* series features middle-aged women wearing clothes that show off as much skin as possible. American women followed and the trend was seen in cities everywhere.

Along with showing off skin, Americans were also showing off body art. Tattoos were becoming so popular that tattoo parlors started cropping up in suburban malls. The Pew

MILITARY FASHIONS

War, on the surface, doesn't seem to bear any relation to fashion or style, yet over the decades it has had a major influence on the clothes we wear. World War II, for example, restricted the amount and type of fabrics that could be used for civilian clothing, and military uniforms from earlier wars have become part of our everyday fashions. In the 2000s, this was more apparent than ever.

Here's a look at some of the most lasting styles:

COATS AND JACKETS

- Eisenhower jacket: This short jacket, with its broad shoulders and narrow waist, was worn by General Dwight D. Eisenhower and American and British troops during World War II. After the war, it became hugely popular in both men and women's clothing.
- Bomber jacket: U.S. fighter pilots in World War II wore this jacket with its zip front, puckered waist-line, and diagonally cut flat-front pockets.
- Pea coat: Sailors started wearing this short double-breasted coat as part of their uniforms in the 1830s.
- Trench coat: These coats, which offer protection from the rain and wind, were named after the trenches in which World War I soldiers fought.
- Duffle coats: Worn by British Royal Navy service-men from the beginning of the twentieth century, they're the only classic men's coat with a hood.
- Epaulettes: This small piece of material on the shoulder was first created as protection against sword blows.

PANTS

- Cargo pants: The British first used large pockets as part of their battle dress uniform in 1938. During World War II, cargo pockets were added to the U.S. Army paratroopers' uniforms to make it easy for them to access ammunition and radios when landing. Cargo pants were brought back by hip-hop groups in the mid–1990s.

- Bell-bottoms: Sailors have been wearing bell-bottomed (wide-legged) pants since the fifteenth century. The wide bottoms made the trousers easy to roll up when the decks got wet and easy to pull off if a sailor went overboard. Bell bottoms were part of the U.S. Navy uniform until 1998.

CAMOUFLAGE

- Camouflage: These patterns help soldiers blend in with the surroundings, whether they are woods or deserts. Camouflage designs have changed quite a bit from the original khaki color worn by soldiers in India in the 1800s. Khaki comes from the Persian word *khak*, which means dust, earth, or mud. Some sources say the Indian soldiers dyed their clothing with natural pigments to disguise dirt, while others say they used tea. Either way, khaki-colored uniforms evolved into the olive drab and brown used by GIs in World War II to the U.S. Woodland (a four-color pattern for temperate and tropical environments) used for the Gulf War. Each branch of the service has its own pattern, and new patterns are constantly being developed.

Research Center, an independent, nonpartisan public opinion research group, reported in 2010 that 38 percent of eighteen to twenty-nine year olds had tattoos compared to only 15 percent of people from forty-six to sixty-four years old. Of those young people who have tattoos, most have more than one. They also have body piercings in places other than the traditional earlobe. The number of tattoos and body piercings and how to deal with them in the job market inspired the title of a book for job searchers in 2009— *Can I Wear My Nose Ring to the Interview?*, by Ellen Gordon Reeves.

SHAPEWEAR

Women gave up foundation garments such as girdles and merry widows back in the 1960s and 1970s, replacing them with the less-constricting control-top pantyhose. But the 2000s brought body shapers back in a new form. Companies such as Spanx produce bodysuits, waist cinchers, and all types of garments designed to slim the body. This shapewear has become the "must have" undergarment for even slender celebrities.

FASHION INFLUENCES FILM

In the 2000s fashion was the focus of both feature films and documentaries. *The Devil Wears Prada* (2006), starring Anne Hathaway and Meryl Streep, was based on Lauren Weisberger's best-selling novel of the same name. It's a look at the world of fashion and magazines through the eyes of a junior assistant to the editor-in-chief of an influential fashion magazine. The documentary *The September Issue* (2009) showed how Anna Wintour, the editor-in-chief of *Vogue*, put together the 2007 fall fashion issue, while *Valentino: The Last Emperor* (2008), looked at the life and haute couture fashion of the legendary designer.

The fashion industry increasingly became the story in the early 2000s. Meryl Streep made a splash in the movie adaption of *The Devil Wears Prada* as a thinly disguised Anna Wintour, editor-in-chief of *Vogue* magazine.

THE INTERPLAY OF FASHION AND TELEVISION

Reality television programs became staples on cable and network channels in the 2000s. Two reality programs about fashion have been hugely successful, running for multiple seasons. *Project Runway* features young designers competing for runway spots at New York's fashion week, and *America's Next Top Model* is a competition for a modeling contract.

Although the women's fashion smash hit *Sex and the City* ended in 2004, reruns are still seen on television. The two subsequent *Sex and the City* movies reinforced the trend for stiletto heels by well-known designers. Scripted television series, such as *Mad Men* and *Gossip Girl*, made their presence felt in the real world.

Gossip Girl, which aired from 2007 to 2012 as a high school soap opera, with its teenage characters wearing crested blazers, mini-kilts, and headbands. The program also featured high-end designer products mixed with more affordable clothes and had a store on its website for fans to buy fashions featured on the show.

Possibly the most influential television series in fashion trends has been *Mad Men*—named after Madison Avenue, the home of advertising companies in the 1950s and 1960s. This cable TV period drama brought back the fashions of the 1960s, including slim-cut menswear and feminine dresses. The show has influenced the lines of New York fashion designers Zac Posen and Michael Kors. The show's costume designer, Janie Bryant, has also become a designer in her own right, creating fashion lines for Brooks Brothers and Banana Republic.

THE ENVIRONMENT AND TECHNOLOGY

While environmentalists had used slogans about protecting the Earth on T-shirts for years, the words turned into action

MAKEUP AND SKIN CARE FOR MEN

By 2009, sales of skin care and grooming products for men were $4.8 billion, twice as much as they had been a decade before. Although makeup for men, from powdered wigs to face patches, has been in fashion at various points in history, during most of the twentieth century, with the exception of the glam rockers, it disappeared. Will it come back? According to one researcher, it may take a generation for color cosmetics for men's eyes, lips, and nails to become widespread.

in the 2000s. Sustainable and eco-friendly fashion includes fabrics made of natural fibers, such as cotton, silk, hemp, and wool. "Organic fabric," which is material that has been grown and manufactured without toxic chemicals, and garments that don't have to be dry-cleaned are also eco-friendly and have become part of the fashion scene.

Companies are also moving toward sustainable lines of fashion through the use of recycled wool and polyester, made from recycled bottles. H&M, for example, launched a sustainable line in 2010, with baby doll-dresses and peasant blouses reminiscent of 1970s fashion. The same year, the Cintas Company, which designs corporate uniforms, introduced tuxedos for banquet staffs that are made of 23 percent-recycled polyester fibers woven from recycled plastic bottles that are machine washable.

Technology also changed the way clothes are labeled. Heat transfer stamps began appearing on T-shirts, cotton turtlenecks, and bras. The stamps print garment information inside the items without using tags.

BURNING MAN

The Burning Man Festival, an annual art celebration that began in 1986, attracts 50,000 people a year. They come to participate in a multitude of activities that vary from year to year, but usually include art installations, parties, seminars on technology and sustainability, and fashion shows. Just being there is like being at an ongoing fashion show as attendees wear all kinds of styles, including their own designs. Fashion designers and manufacturers have captured the mood and creative energy of the festival with metallic and faded-neon makeup, perfume, and footwear that fashion magazines have called "Park Ave meets Burning Man sandals."

FASHION TREND-MAKERS

Even before her husband took office, Michelle Obama gained attention for her impeccable fashion taste, and once she became first lady, she became known as a mix-and-match master. She wears mass-market brands like J. Crew and clothes from young designers like Jason Wu and Thakoon. Her unique style has made Michelle Obama the First Lady of Fashion.

Pop artist Lady Gaga has a style that's exclusively hers. Her 2008 debut album, *The Fame*, was just the start of a spectacular presence. Lady Gaga combined dance, singing, and fashion to create performance art. Her outfits have ranged from a jacket made of Kermit the Frogs to a meat dress to super high shoes. Lady Gaga's style is one of personal expression, with each outfit more extraordinary than the one worn before. In 2011, Gaga received the Fashion Icon Award from the Council of Fashion Designers of America "for being a fashion revolutionary impacting style today."

As have earlier presidents' wives, First Lady Michelle Obama has influenced fashion trends.

Teenage pop sensation Justin Bieber's leather jackets, high-top tennis shoes, and mop-head hairstyle became the style for young men in 2010.

CELEBRITY FASHION LINES

Celebrities, from actors to singers to sports figures, have often set trends or served as fashion icons. Fans often follow their leads. Rather than just endorsing a certain brand, a number

Perhaps no one has made more outré statements about fashion in the twenty-first century than Lady Gaga, known not least for her dress made of meat, though here dressed and coiffed with relative decorum.

of celebrities started their own fashion lines in the late 1990s and the 2000s. They included Sean "P. Diddy" Combs, Jennifer Lopez, Sarah Jessica Parker, Venus Williams, Mary-Kate and Ashley Olsen, Justin Timberlake, Beyoncé Knowles, Ashley Judd, Victoria Beckham, and Gwen Stefani.

One of the most successful celebrity fashion lines belongs to Jessica Simpson, the pop singer and star of the reality TV show *Newlyweds Nick and Jessica*, which ran from 2003–2005. Simpson's clothing line started with footwear and then expanded to sportswear, dresses, handbags, fashion jewelry, intimate apparel, and fragrances. Retail sales from her line reached $1 billion in 2012, and with the launch of her maternity line that same year, sales are expected to grow even higher.

PLUS-SIZE FASHION

Despite all the diets promoted on television and the Internet, Americans of all ages have been gaining weight. According to the Center for Disease Control, more than 18 percent of adolescents age twelve to nineteen years old were obese in 2007 to 2008 compared to only 5 percent in 1976 to 1980. Over one-third of adults are obese and another third are overweight.

Lane Bryant and other stores have offered plus-size clothes since the 1920s, but finding fashionable clothes for the average overweight American has been difficult until recently, when a number of designers and mass-market stores began catering to larger Americans. With the recession of 2008, plus sizes have been one area that has shown growth. Some brands stopped selling their plus sizes in stores, offering the larger sizes online only. But other brands have found plus size clothing to be a lucrative market, especially with celebrities such as Oprah Winfrey, Queen Latifah, and model Emme showcasing fashionable outfits.

Fashion magazines such as *Glamour* and *Vogue Italia* have featured plus-size models, and several modeling agencies now have plus-size divisions. For many women who have struggled with their body image from a young age, seeing full-figured women modeling the latest fashions has given them a new sense of self-esteem.

LIVING FASHION

Fashion has changed considerably over the decades, from the constrained clothing of the 1950s to the loose, casual attire of the last part of the 1990s and the first decade of the 2000s. And while fashion has changed, it has also revisited previous eras for ideas. It's easier than ever to see the fashions of the past as they were actually worn by watching period television and movies. Some of these programs are described in the text. Here are some more that you might want to take a look at:

- *I Love Lucy* (1951–1957)
- *The Dick Van Dyke Show* (1961–1966)
- *The Avengers* (1961–1969)
- *That Girl* (1966–1971)
- *The Brady Bunch* (1969–1974)
- *The Mary Tyler Moore Show* (1970–1977)
- *Welcome Back Kotter* (1975–1979)
- *Hill Street Blues* (1981–1987)
- *Cheers* (1982–1993)
- *The Cosby Show* (1984–1992)
- *Beverly Hills, 90210* (1990–2000)
- *Buffy the Vampire Slayer* (1997–2003)
- *The West Wing* (1999–2006)

Although produced and viewed decades after the time they portray, *Happy Days* (1974–1984) shows the fashions and attitudes of teenagers of the 1950s and 1960s and *That '70s Show* (1998–2006) does the same for the 1970s.

John Hughes's films, including *Sixteen Candles* (1984), *The*

Breakfast Club (1985), *Ferris Bueller's Day Off* (1986) and *Pretty in Pink* (1986) all reflected the styles actually worn by teens during the 1980s.

DECADE IN REVIEW

By the early 2000s fashion had moved a long way from the 1950s, when the dictates of French designers and fashion magazines determined what was in style. Today, fashion trends happen with a click of the mouse as bloggers, social media, and other technologies enable people to share their favorite looks. Popular culture, especially music and television, are essential in creating trends, but more than ever, everyone plays a part in the fashion process when they decide what to buy and to wear.

Designers are still influential, as are trend designers, who rely on their labels to promote a certain style. Luxury designer fashion appeals to and is worn by socialites, celebrities, power players in business and industry, and those who want to let everyone know they can afford the best. The red carpet question at every awards ceremony is always, "Who are you wearing?" For most celebrities, the answer is a well-known designer's name. In fact, by wearing a certain dress, a celebrity can bring a new designer a huge amount of publicity and start him or her onto the path of fame and fortune. Social media can do the same, and many young designers use the Internet to promote themselves and their clothes.

Although this book is divided by decades, fashion doesn't change on a strict timeline. Some trends overlap from one decade to the next, others reappear a decade or two later. Certain styles, such as the "little black dress" and jeans, have become classics, and are always a part of the fashion scene. The interplay of fashion and culture is fascinating. As you decide what to wear each day, take a moment to think about how both of them have affected your choice.

Notes

CHAPTER 1

p. 7, "The U.S. government . . .": "American Fashion Goes to War," in *American Decades*, 2001, www.encyclopedia.com/doc/1G2-3468301492.html.

p. 9, "Dior said . . .": Valerie Steel, *Fifty Years of Fashion* (New Haven, CT: Yale University Press), 15.

p. 12, "Designers Bonnie Cashin, . . .": "Clothing and Fashion," in Dictionary of American History, 2003, *Encyclopedia.com*, www.encyclopedia.com/doc/1G2-3401800875.html.

p. 12, "Givenchy said it is . . .": Valerie Steel, *Fifty Years of Fashion*, 41.

pp. 15–16, "Every kid wanted . . .": Rita Lang Kleinfelder, *When We Were Young: A Baby-Boomer Yearbook* (New York: Prentice Hall General Reference, 1993) 164.

p. 17, "These codes called . . .": Jeanne Rogers, "Dress Code For Pupils Proposed to Principals: Buffalo Official Says Clothes Worn To School Influence General Behavior," *The Washington Post and Times Herald*, February 26, 1957.

p. 18, "In August 1959, . . .": "Real Gone Garb for Fall, Beat but Neat," in *Life*, August 3, 1959, 48–49, http://books.google.com/books?id=80kEAAAAM BAJ&pg=PP1&dq=Life+August+3,+1959&hl=en&ei=0zM8TvqsNcTu0 gHqpKDVAw&sa=X&oi=book_result&ct=result&resnum=1&ved=0CCs Q6AEwADgK#v=onepage&q=Life%20August%203%2C%201959&f=true.

CHAPTER 2

p. 23, "Cosmetic manufacturers followed . . .": *Harper's Bazaar*, May, 1966, 26–27.

p. 25, "One example is "The Souper Dress" . . .": Valerie Steel (*Fifty Years of Fashion* New Haven, CT: Yale University Press) 61.

p. 25, "Saint Laurent used . . .": Suzy Menkes, "The Return of Marilyn, the Reincarnation of Warhol : Pop Art Fashion Roars Back," *New York Times*, April 3, 2001, www.nytimes.com/2001/04/03/style/03iht-fash_ed2_html?pagewanted= print.

p. 25, "Inexpensive, with ...": Kathleen Paton, "Paper Dresses," in *The Berg Companion to Fashion*, ed. Valerie Steele (Oxford, New York: Berg, 2010) 550–551.

p. 28, "Their new style ...": "Mod Styles and the London Scene," in *Fashion, Costume, and Culture: Clothing, Headwear, Body Decorations, and Footwear through the Ages*, 2004. *Encyclopedia.com*, www.encyclopedia.com/doc/1G2-3425500585.html.

CHAPTER 3

p. 37, "In the 1920s, economist ...": Catherine Valenti, "Do Short Skirts Really Mean Better Times?" *ABC News*, January 17, 2003, http://abcnews.go.com/Business/story?id=86787&page=1.

p. 37, "She wrote ...": Valerie Steele, *Fifty Years of Fashion* (New Haven, CT: Yale University Press) 86.

p. 38, "Young black designer ...": Dennita Sewell, "Burrows, Stephen," in *Encyclopedia of Clothing and Fashion*, ed. Valerie Steele, Detroit: Charles Scribner's Sons, 2005, 203–204.

p. 38, "According to *Women's* ...": Jessica Iredale, "The Americans Conquer Versailles," in *WWD-100 Years*, October 30, 2010, 204.

p. 39, "He asked Levi Strauss ...": Phyllis Tortora, "Snapshot: Jeans," in *Encyclopedia of World Dress and Fashion*, Vol. 3, *The United States and Canada*, ed. Phyllis G. Tortora (Oxford, UK: University Press, 2010) 64–65.

p. 39, "That fabric was made ...": "The Moment," *New York Times*, January 16, 2011.

p. 41, "The warm-up suit ...": Kelly Boyer Sagert, *The 1970s: American Popular Culture Through History* (Westport, CT: Greenwood Press, 2007) 98.

p. 44, "When Westwood realized ...": Ann T. Kellogg, Amy T. Peterson, Stefani Bay, and Natalie Swindell, in *In an Influential Fashion: An Encyclopedia of Nineteenth- and Twentieth-Century Fashion Designers and Retailers Who Transformed Dress* (Westport, CT: Greenwood Press, 2002) 315–317.

p. 48, "In a 1976 article ...": "Goodbye, Love Beads. Hello, Watch Chain," *Annual Banking Issue, Forbes*, July 1, 1976, 19.

p. 48, "In the *Women's* ...": Judy Klemesrud, "Behind the Best Sellers, John T. Molloy," *New York Times Book Review*, March 12, 1978, http://select.nytimes.com/gst/abstract.html?res=F00913FE3D5513728DDDAB0994DB405B888BF1D3&scp=1&sq=behind%20the%20best%20sellers%20John%20Molloy&st=cse.

p. 48, "Liz Claiborne said ...": Lisa Lockwood, "The Liz Blitz," *WWD-100 Years*, October 30, 2010, 204.

p. 49, "By chance, I ...": Kennedy Fraser, *The Fashionable Mind, Reflections on Fashion, 1970-1982* (Boston: D.R. Godine, 1985) xi.

p. 49, "Fashion marketers became ...": Jill Ross, and Rod Harradine, "I'm not wearing that! Branding and young children," *Journal of Fashion Marketing and Management*, Vol. 8, Number 1 (2004): 11–26.

p. 50, "Klein often said . . .": Bonnie English, *A Cultural History of Fashion in the 20th Century: From the Catwalk to the Sidewalk* (New York: Berg, 2007) 72.

p. 51, "He said . . . :" Margit J. Mayer, "U.S. Lifestyle," in *Icons of Fashion, The 20th Century*, ed. Gerda Buxbaum (NewYork: Prestel, 1999) 132.

CHAPTER 4

p. 52, "What was considered fashionable . . . ": Phyllis Tortora, "Types and Properties of Fashionable Dress," in *Encyclopedia of World Dress and Fashion*, Vol. 3, *The United States and Canada*, ed. Phyllis G. Tortora, Oxford, UK: Oxford University Press, 2010, 63.

p. 55, "The most important . . . ": Alison Lurie, *The Language of Clothes* (New York: 1st Owl Books ed., Henry Holt, 2000) 164.

p. 55, "The top logo was . . . ": José Blanco F., Scott Leff, Ann T. Kellogg, and Lynn W. Payne. "Women's Fashions," in *The Greenwood Encyclopedia of Clothing through American History, 1900 to the Present*, Vol. 2 (Westport, CT: Greenwood Press, 2008) 225.

p. 55, "The frayed seams and . . . ":, Ingrid Loschek, *When Clothes Become Fashion: Design and Innovation Systems* (Oxford, UK: Berg, 2009) 105.

p. 56, "Air Jordans were so . . . ": José Blanco F., Scott Leff, Ann T. Kellogg, and Lynn W. Payne, "The Social Significance of Dress," in *The Greenwood Encyclopedia of Clothing through American History, 1900 to the Present*, Vol. 2, 112.

p. 56, "Nike's 1988 advertising": www.nikebiz.com/company_overview/time-line/.

p. 59, "In 1985, the Council . . . ": www.cfda.com/past-winners/.

p. X, "His fashions became . . . ": Patricia A. Cunningham, Heather Mangine, and Andrew Reilly, "Television and Fashion in the 1980s," in *Twentieth-century American Fashion*, eds. Linda Welters and Patricia A. Cunningham (Oxford, UK: Berg, 2005) 225.

p. 62, "Cintra Wilson . . .": Cintra Wilson, "You Just Can't Kill It," *New York Times*, September 17, 2008, www.nytimes.com/2008/09/18/fashion/18GOTH. html?scp=9&sq=Cintra%20Wilson&st=cse.

p. 63, "To fashion historians . . . ": Valerie Steele, and Jennifer Park, *Gothic: Dark Glamour* (New York: Yale University Press and The Fashion Institute of Technology, 2008) 6.

p. 64, "Fashion is change . . . ": Christa Worthington, "Keeping up with Kaiser Karl," in *Women's Wear Daily*, February 21, 1986.

CHAPTER 5

p. 65, "Casual Fridays became . . .": Daniel Akst, "The Culture of Money; Foulard and Rep, Rest in Peace? Not So Fast!" *New York Times*, December 6, 1998, www. nytimes.com/1998/12/06/business/the-culture-of-money-foulard-and-rep-rest-in-peace-not-so-fast.html?scp=75&sq=office+dress+codes&st=nyt.

p. 66, "As the lines . . .": "A Glimmer of Glam Clothes for Club-Hopping and Concertgoing Are Sleek and Sparkly," *Rocky Mountain News*, Denver, CO., November 21, 1999.

p. 68, "In 1998, rap outsold . . . ": Christopher John Farley, "Music: Hip-Hop Nation," in *Time*, February 8, 1999, www.time.com/time/magazine/article/0,9171,990164,00.html.

p. 69, "Female rapper Lil' Kim . . . ": Van Dyke Lewis, "Hip-Hop Fashion," in *The Berg Companion to Fashion*, ed. Valerie Steel (Oxford, New York: Berg, 2010) 416.

p. 69, "Several months before . . .": "The Star-Spangled Manner," *WWD*, December 7, 1999. www.wwd.com/fashion-news/article-1075374.

p. 73, "Goth fashion has . . .": Robert Seidman, NCIS Voted America's All-Time Favorite TV Show, May 5, 2011, http://tvbythenumbers.zap2it.com/2011/05/05/ncis-voted-americas-all-time-favorite-tv-show-two-and-a-half-men-bones-house-several-current-shows-rank/91686/.

p. 74, *Sex and the City* made . . . ": Ruth La Ferla, "Film and Fashion: Just Friends," *New York Times*, March 3, 2010.

p. 74, "Trends were also set . . .": Valerie Steele (*Fifty Years of Fashion*, New Haven, CT: Yale University Press, 1997) 143.

p. 74, "These women were . . .": Barbara Rudolph, Anne Constable, Lenora Dodsworth, Edward M. Gomez, "Marketing Beauty and The Bucks," *Time*, October 7, 1991, www.time.com/time/magazine/article/0,9171,973984,00.html.

p. 75, "However, parents of teenagers . . . ": Andrea Peterson, "Legal beat: parents spur laws against tattoos for kids," *Wall Street Journal*, September 16, 1996.

CHAPTER 6

p. 76, "H&M opened its . . . ": Sarah Raper Larenaudie, "Inside the H&M Fashion Machine," *Time*, February 16, 2004, www.time.com/time/printout/0,8816,993352,00.html.

p. 82, "The Pew Research Center . . .": Millennials Confident Connected Open to Change, www.pewresearch.org/millennials.

p. 85, "By 2009, sales . . . ": Andrew Adam Newman, "Men's Cosmetics Becoming a Bull Market," *New York Times*, September 1, 2010, www.nytimes.com/2010/09/02/fashion/02skin.html?scp=1&sq=Men%E2%80%99s%20Cosmetics%20Becoming%20a%20Bull%20Market,&st=cse.

p. 85, "According to one . . . ": Andrew Adam Newman, "Men's Cosmetics Becoming a Bull Market," *New York Times*, September 1, 2010, www.nytimes.com/2010/09/02/fashion/02skin.html?scp=1&sq=Men%E2%80%99s%20Cosmetics%20Becoming%20a%20Bull%20Market,&st=cse.

p. 85, "The same year . . .": "Cintas Introduces Machine-Washable Tuxedos," *Business Wire* October 18, 2010.

p. 86, "Fashion designers and manufacturers . . .": Monica Corcoran Harel, "Desert fires: the smoky looks and scents of burning man come to L.A," in *Los Angeles Magazine*, August 2011, 64.

p. 86, "In 2001, Gaga . . .": "2011 CFDA FASHION AWARDS NOMINEES & HONOREES ANNOUNCED," www.cfda.com/2011-cfda-fashion-awards-nominees-honorees-announced/.

p. 89, "Retail sales from her . . .": Lisa Lockwood, "Jessica Simpson: A Real, Live Girl," *WWD Special Report Issue,* March 28, 2011, www.wwd.com/eyescoop/jessica-simpson-a-real-live-girl-3565797#/article/eyescoop/jessica-simpson-a-real-girl-3565797?full=true.

p. 89, "According to the Center . . .": Cynthia Ogden and Margaret Carroll, M.S.P.H, "Prevalence of Obesity Among Children and Adolescents: United States, Trends 1963–1965 Through 2007–2008," *NCHS Health E-Stat,* www.cdc.gov/nchs/data/hestat/obesity_child_07_08/obesity_child_07_08.htm.

p. 89, "Over one-third . . .": www.cdc.gov/nchs/fastats/ovewt.htm.

Further Information

BOOKS

Stadler, Erika. *Fashion 101—A Crash Course in Clothing*. San Francisco, CA: Zest Books, 2008.

Waterman, Lauren. *The Teen Vogue Handbook—An Insider's Guide to Careers in Fashion*. New York: Razorbill, 2009.

WEBSITES

Ask Men
www.askmen.com

Daily Fashion
www.dailyfashion.com

The Museum at the Fashion Institute of Technology's Online Collection
fashionmuseum.fitnyc.edu

Fashion Television
www.fashiontelevision.com

Full Frontal Fashion
www.fullfrontalfashion.com (redirects to sundancechannel.com)

The Metropolitan Museum of Art's Costume Institue
www.metmuseum.org/research/curatorial%20research/the%20costume%20institute

The Museum of Costume
www.museumofcostume.co.uk/default.aspx

Style Magazine
www.style.com/magazine

Bibliography

Note that citations from Berg publications, including the *Encyclopedia of World Dress and Fashion, The Berg Companion to Fashion,* and *Twentieth-century American Fashion* can be found in the Berg Fashion Library online, which can be accessed through public and university libraries.

"2011 CFDA FASHION AWARDS NOMINEES & HONOREES ANNOUNCED," www.cfda.com/2011-cfda-fashion-awards-nominees-honorees-announced/.

"A Glimmer of Glam Clothes for Club-Hopping and Concertgoing Are Sleek and Sparkly." *Rocky Mountain News,* Denver, CO. November 21, 1999.

"American Chic in Fashion." *Time,* March 22, 1976. www.time.com/time/magazine/article/0,9171,911783,00.html.

"American Fashion Goes to War." American Decades. 2001. *Encyclopedia.com.*

"Cintas Introduces Machine-Washable Tuxedos." *Business Wire,* October 18, 2010.

Clifford, Stephanie, "Plus-Size Revelation: Bigger Women have Cash, Too." *New York Times,* June 18, 2010, www.nytimes.com/2010/06/19/business/19plus.html?_r=1&scp=1&sq=plus%20sizes&st=cse.

"Clothing, 1980–2003." *Fashion, Costume, and Culture: Clothing, Headwear, Body Decorations, and Footwear through the Ages.* Vol. 5: *Modern World Part II: 1946-2003,* ed. Sara Pendergast and Tom Pendergast. Detroit: UXL, 2004, 975–980.

"Clothing and Fashion." Dictionary of American History. 2003. *Encyclopedia.com.* www.encyclopedia.com/doc/1G2-3401800875.html.

"Clothing for Youth," American Decades. 2001. *Encyclopedia.com.* www.encyclopedia.com/doc/1G2-3468303034.html.

"Go-Go Boots." *Fashion, Costume, and Culture: Clothing, Headwear, Body Decorations, and Footwear through the Ages.* Vol. 5: *Modern World Part II: 1946-2003,* ed. by Sara Pendergast and Tom Pendergast. Detroit: UXL, 2004, 963–964.

"Millennials Confident Connected Open to Change." www.pewresearch.org/ millennials.

"Past Winners." Council of Fashion Designers of America. www.cfda.com/ past.

"Real Gone Garb for Fall, Beat but Neat," *Life*, August 3, 1959, 48–49.

"The Star-Spangled Manner." *WWD.COM*. December 7, 1999, www.wwd. com/fashion-news/article-1075374.

"The Moment." *New York Times*, January 16, 2011.

Agins, Teri. *The End of Fashion*. New York: William Morrow & Co. Inc., 1999.

Akst, Daniel. "The Culture of Money; Foulard and Rep, Rest in Peace? Not So fast!" *New York Times*, December 6, 1998, www.nytimes.com/1998/12/06/ business/the-culture-of-money-foulard-and-rep-rest-in-peace-not-so-fast. html?scp=75&sq=office+dress+codes&st=nyt.

Baldaia, Suzanne. "Space Age Fashion," In *Twentieth-Century American Fashion*, edited by Linda Welters and Patricia A. Cunningham, Oxford, UK: Berg, 2005, 169–189.

Batchelor, Bob, and Scott F. Stoddart. *The 1980s: American Pop Culture Through History*. Westport, CT: Greenwood Press, 2007.

Bell, Jennie, "Readers' Choice: What Went on in Fashion." *Footwear News Issue*, December 20, 2010. www.wwd.com/footwear-news/readers-choice-what-went-on-in-fashion-3406015.

Bensimon, Kelly Killoren. *American Style*. New York: Assouline Publishing, Inc., 2004.

Blanco F., José, Scott Leff, Ann T. Kellogg, and Lynn W. Payne. "Women's Fashion." In *The Greenwood Encyclopedia of Clothing through American History, 1900 to the Present*, Vol. 2. Westport, CT: Greenwood Press, 2008, 179–246.

——. "The Social Significance of Dress." *The Greenwood Encyclopedia of Clothing through American History, 1900 to the Present*, Vol. 2, Westport, CT: Greenwood Press, 2008, 1–156.

Broeske, Pat H. "American Bandstand." In *St. James Encyclopedia of Popular Culture*, Vol. 1, ed. Sara Pendergast and Tom Pendergast. Detroit: St. James Press, 2000, 65–67.

Bruzzi, Stella. "Film and Fashion." In *Encyclopedia of Clothing and Fashion*, Vol. 2, ed. Valerie Steele. Detroit: Charles Scribner's Sons, 2005, 82–86.

Buckland, Sandra Stansbery. "Writing about Fashions." *Encyclopedia of World Dress and Fashion*, Vol. 3, *The United States and Canada*, ed. Phyllis G. Tortora. New York: Oxford University Press, 2010, 122–127.

Chandler, Robin M., and Nuri Chandler-Smith. "Flava in Ya Gear: Transgressive Politics and the Influence of Hip-Hop on Contemporary Fashion." *Twentieth-century American Fashion*, ed. Linda Welters and Patricia A. Cunningham. Oxford, UK: Berg, 2005, 229–254.

Chang, Angel. "Sport Shoes." In *Encyclopedia of Clothing and Fashion*, Vol. 3, ed. Valerie Steele. Detroit: Charles Scribner's Sons, 2005, 213–216.

Coronado, ViBrina. "Tennis Shoes/Sneakers." In *St. James Encyclopedia of Popular Culture*, Vol. 4, ed. Sara Pendergast and Tom Pendergast. Detroit, MI: St. James Press, 2000, 637–638.

Cunningham, Patricia A. "Dressing for Success: The Re-Suiting of Corporate America in the 1970s." In *Twentieth-century American Fashion*, ed. Linda Welters and Patricia A. Cunningham. Oxford, UK: Berg, 2005, 191–208.

Cunningham, Patricia. "Television." In *Encyclopedia of World Dress and Fashion*, Vol. 3, *The United States and Canada*, edited by Phyllis G. Tortora. New York: Oxford University Press, 2010, 283–288.

Cunningham, Patricia A., Heather Mangine, and Andrew Reilly. "Television and Fashion in the 1980s." In *Twentieth-century American Fashion*, edited by Linda Welters and Patricia A. Cunningham. Oxford, UK: Berg, 2005, 209–228.

Demographic Profile America's Gen X, Metropolitan Life, www.metlife.com/assets/cao/mmi/publications/Profiles/mmi-gen-x-demographic-profile.pdf.

Douglas, Susan J. "Girls 'n' spice: all things nice?" *The Nation*, August 25, 1997. English, Bonnie. *A Cultural History of Fashion in the 20th Century: From the Catwalk to the Sidewalk*. Oxford, U.K.: Berg, 2007.

Farley, Christopher John. "Music: Hip-Hop Nation." In *Time*, February 8, 1999 www.time.com/time/magazine/article/0,9171,990164,00.html.

Farrell-Beck, Jane and Jean Parsons. *20th-Century Dress in the United States*. New York: Fairchild Publications, 2007.

Flegal, Katherine M., Margaret D. Carroll, Cynthia L. Ogden, Lester R. Curtin. "Original Contribution Prevalence and Trends in Obesity Among US Adults, 1999–2008." *JAMA*. 2010;303(3):235-241. January 13, 2010. http://jama.ama-assn.org/content/303/3/235.full?ijkey=ijKHq6YbJn3Oo&keytype=ref&siteid=amajnls.

Flores, Gerald, "Media Wave: The Next Fashion Trendsetter." *Footwear News Issue*, August 2, 2010, www.wwd.com/footwear-news/media-wave-the-next-fashion-trendsetters-3199529#/article/footwear-news/media-wave-the-next-fashion-trendsetters-3199529?full=true.

Fraser, Kennedy. *The Fashionable Mind: Reflections on Fashion, 1970-1982*. Boston: D. R. Godine, 1985.

Gibbs, Nancy. "The Pill at 50: Sex, Freedom and Paradox." *Time*, April 22, 2010.

Ginsberg, Merle. "TV Ups The Fashion Quotient," *WWD.com*, July 28, 2000, www.wwd.com/fashion-news/article-1196941.

Greatrex, Tom. "Coat." In *Encyclopedia of Clothing and Fashion*, Vol. 1, ed. Valerie Steele. Detroit: Charles Scribner's Sons, 2005, 272–274.

Gross, Michael. "Supermodels." In *The Berg Companion to Fashion*, ed. Valerie Steele. Oxford, U.K.: Berg, 2010, 663–665.

Grossman, Perry. "Punk." In *St. James Encyclopedia of Popular Culture*. Vol. 4, ed. Sara Pendergast and Tom Pendergast. Detroit, MI: St. James Press, 2000, 142–145.

Harel, Monica Corcoran. "Desert fires: the smoky looks and scents of burning man come to L.A." In *Los Angeles Magazine*, August, 2011, 64.

Harris, Rachel Lee. "Lady Gaga Is Fantastic." *New York Times*, July 4, 2010. www.nytimes.com/2010/07/05/arts/music/05arts-LADYGAGAISFA_BRF.html?sq=Lady Gaga&st=cse&scp=28&pagewanted=print.

Hilger, Jan. "The Apparel Industry." In *Encyclopedia of World Dress and Fashion*, Vol. 8, *West Europe*, ed. Lise Skov, New York: Oxford University Press, 2010, 111-117.

Iredale, Jessica. "The Americans Conquer Versailles." In *WWD-100 Years*, October 30, 2010.

Jacobs, Alexandra. "Smooth Moves." *New Yorker*, March 28, 2011.

Kaiser, Susan and Ryan Looysen. "Antifashion." In *Encyclopedia of World Dress and Fashion*, Vol. 3, *The United States and Canada*, ed. Phyllis G. Tortora, New York: Oxford University Press, 2010, 160–170.

Kawamura, Yuniya. "The Fashion Industry." In *Encyclopedia of World Dress and Fashion*, Vol. 10, *Global Perspectives*, edited by Joanne B. Eicher, 191–203. Oxford, U.K.: Oxford University Press, 2010, 191–203.

Kellogg, Ann T., Amy T. Peterson, Stefani Bay, and Natalie Swindell. In *In an Influential Fashion: An Encyclopedia of Nineteenth- and Twentieth-Century Fashion Designers and Retailers Who Transformed Dress*. Westport, CT: Greenwood Press, 2002, 315–317.

Kennedy, Shirley. "Pucci, Emilio." In *The Berg Companion to Fashion*, ed. Valerie Steele, Oxford, U.K.: Berg, 2010, 579–581.

Kleinfelder, Rita Lang. *When We Were Young: A Baby-Boomer Yearbook.* New York: Prentice Hall General Reference, 1993.

La Ferla, Ruth. "Film and Fashion: Just Friends." *New York Times,* March 3, 2010, www.nytimes.com/2010/03/04/fashion/04COSTUME.html?scp=1&sq=Film+and+Fashion%3A+Just+Friends&st=nyt.

Larenaudie, Sarah Raper. "Inside the H&M Fashion Machine." *Time,* February 16, 2004, www.time.com/time/printout/0,8816,993352,00.html.

Larocca, Amy. "Park Avenue Jesus!" *New York,* August 23, 2010.

Lewis, Van Dyk. "Afrocentric Fashion." In *The Berg Companion to Fashion,* ed. Valerie Steele, Oxford, U.K.: Berg, 2010, 14–17.

——— "Hip-Hop Fashion." In *The Berg Companion to Fashion,* ed. Valerie Steele, Oxford, U.K.: Berg, 2010, 413–417.

Lockwood, Lisa. "Jessica Simpson: A Real, Live Girl." *WWD Special Report Issue,* March 28, 2011, www.wwd.com/eyescoop/jessica-simpson-a-real-live-girl-3565797#/article/eyescoop/jessica-simpson-a-real-girl-3565797?full=true.

———. "The Liz Blitz." *WWD-100 Years,* October 30, 2010.

Loschek, Ingrid. *When Clothes Become Fashion: Design and Innovation Systems.* Oxford, U.K.: Berg, 2009.

Loschek, Ingrid. "Twentieth-Century Fashion." *Encyclopedia of Clothing and Fashion.* Vol. 3, ed. Valerie Steele. Detroit: Charles Scribner's Sons, 2005, 348–353.

Lowe, Elizabeth. "Class." *Encyclopedia of World Dress and Fashion,* Vol. 3, *The United States and Canada,* edited by Phyllis G. Tortora. New York: Oxford University Press, 2010, 233–239.

Lurie, Alison. *The Language of Clothes.* 1st Owl Books ed., New York: Henry Holt, 2000.

McDermott, Catherine. "Diana, Princess of Wales." In *Encyclopedia of Clothing and Fashion.* Vol. 1, ed. Valerie Steele, Detroit, MI: Charles Scribner's Sons, 2005, 363–364.

Marion, Peggy. "Travolta's fashion appeal: staying alive?" *Daily News Record,* July 26, 1983.

Mayer, Margit J., "U.S. Lifestyle," In *Icons of Fashion: the 20th Century,* ed. Gerda Buxbaum. New York: Prestel, 1999, 132.

Melinkoff, Ellen. *What We Wore: An Offbeat Social History of Women's Clothing, 1950 to 1980.* New York: Quill, 1984.

Mendes, Valerie, and Amy de la Haye. *Fashion since 1900*. 2nd ed. New York: Thames & Hudson, Inc., 2010.

Milbank, Caroline Rennolds. "Space Age." *Icons of Fashion: the 20th Century*, ed. Gerda Buxbaum. New York: Prestel, 1999, 88–89.

Montrose, Natasha. "Hoodies Gain Iconic Status." *WWD*, January 28, 2010, www.wwd.com/markets-news/hoodie-gain-iconic-status-2438322.

Newman, Andrew Adam. "Men's Cosmetics Becoming a Bull Market." *New York Times*, September 1, 2010, www.nytimes.com/2010/09/02/fashion/02skin.html?scp=1&sq=Men%E2%80%99s%20Cosmetics%20Becoming%20a%20Bull%20Market,&st=cse.

Nike Timeline. www.nikebiz.com/company_overview/timeline/.

Ogden, Cynthia, and Margaret Carroll, M.S.P.H. "Prevalence of Obesity Among Children and Adolescents: United States, Trends 1963-1965 Through 2007-2008." *NCHS Health E-Stat*, www.cdc.gov/nchs/data/hestat/obesity_child_07_08/obesity_child_07_08.htm.

Ogunnaike, Lola. "Christina Aguilera, That Dirrty Girl, Cleans Up Real Nice." *New York Times*, July 30, 2006, www.nytimes.com/2006/07/30/arts/30ogun.html?scp=8&sq=Christina%20Aguilera&st=cse.

Ono, Yumiko, and Wendy Bounds. "Fashion: Army Pants With Pounchy Pockets Storm Fashion World." *Wall Street Journal*, July 9, 1998.

Oxoby, Marc. *Popular Culture of the 1990s: American Popular Culture Through History*. Westport, CT: Greenwood Press, 2003.

Paton, Kathleen. "Paper Dresses." *The Berg Companion to Fashion*, ed. Valerie Steele. Oxford, U.K.: Berg, 2010, 550–551.

Polhemus, Ted. "Street Style." *Encyclopedia of Clothing and Fashion*, Vol. 3, ed. Valerie Steele. Detroit, MI: Charles Scribner's Sons, 2005, 225–229.

Postrel, Virginia. "Fashion as Art: Fashion Week's move to Lincoln Center reflects a growing recognition of style as culture." *Wall Street Journal*, September 11, 2010.

Reid-Walsh, Jacqueline, and Claudia A. Mitchell. "SPICE GIRLS." *Girl Culture (Two Volumes): An Encyclopedia*. Santa Barbara, CA: Greenwood Press, 2007, 551–553.

Rielly, Edward J. *The 1960s: American Popular Culture Through History*. Westport, CT: Greenwood Press, 2003.

Rogers, Jeanne. "Dress Code For Pupils Proposed to Principals: Buffalo Official Says Clothes Worn To School Influence General Behavior." *Washington*

Post and Times Herald (1954–1959), February 26, 1957.

Rosenberg, Merri. "Next Generation; Cover-Up in Irvington: Dress Code at Schools." *New York Times*, May 27, 2001. www.nytimes.com/2001/05/27/nyregion/next-generation-cover-up-in-irvington-dress-code-at-schools.html?scp=74&sq=office+dress+codes&st=nyt.

Ross, Jill, and Rod Harradine. "I'm not wearing that! Branding and young children." *Journal of Fashion Marketing and Management*, Vol. 8, No.1 (2004): 11–26.

Rudolph, Barbara, Anne Constable, Lenora Dodsworth, Edward M. Gomez. "Marketing Beauty and The Bucks." *Time*, October 7, 1991, www.time.com/time/magazine/article/0,9171,973984,00.html.

Sagert, Kelly Boyer. *The 1970s: American Popular Culture Through History*. Westport, CT: Greenwood Press, 2007.

Sales, Nancy Jo. "Donna Karan's Journey." *Harper's Bazaar*, September 21, 2010, www.harpersbazaar.com/fashion/fashion-articles/donna-karan-interview-1010.

Schwartz, Benjamin. "Fashion in Dark Times." *Atlantic*, April 24, 2009, www.theatlantic.com/magazine/archive/2009/06/fashion-in-dark-times/7440/.

Sewell, Dennita. "Burrows, Stephen." In *Encyclopedia of Clothing and Fashion*, Vol. 1, ed. Valerie Steele. New York: Charles Scribner's Sons, 2005, 203–204.

Shih, Candice. "Women and their jeans: a love story." *Orange County Register*, Santa Ana, CA, November 11, 2009.

Stalder, Erica. *Fashion 101, A Crash Course in Clothing*. San Francisco: Zest Books, 2008.

"The Star-Spangled Manner." *WWD*, December 7, 1999. www.wwd.com/fashion-news/article-1075374.

Steele, Valerie. *Fifty Years of Fashion*. New Haven, CT: Yale University Press, 1997.

Steele, Valerie, and Jennifer Park. *Gothic: Dark Glamour*. New York: Yale University Press and The Fashion Institute of Technology, 2008.

Steele, Valerie, and Gillion Carrara. "Italian Fashion." In *The Berg Companion to Fashion*, ed. Valerie Steele. Oxford, U.K.: Berg, 2010, 430–432.

Steinhauer, Jennifer, and Constance C. R. White. "Women's New Relationship With Fashion." *New York Times*, August 5, 1996, www.nytimes.com/1996/08/05/business/women-s-new-relationship-with-fashion.html?scp=71&sq=office+dress+codes&st=nyt.

Stone, Elaine. *The Dynamics of Fashion.* 3rd ed. New York: Fairchild Books, 2008.

Tan, Cheryl Lu-Lien. "Style: The Keepers in Your Closet." *Wall Street Journal*, December 27, 2007.

Tonchi, Stefano. "Military Style." In *The Berg Companion to Fashion,* ed. Valerie Steele. Oxford: New York: Berg, 2010, 507–508.

Tortora, Phyllis G. "Iconic Figures in Western Fashion." *Encyclopedia of World Dress and Fashion,* Vol. 10, *Global Perspectives,* ed. Joanne B. Eicher. New York: Oxford University Press, 2010, 171–174.

———. "Introduction to Fashion." *Encyclopedia of World Dress and Fashion,* Vol. 3, *The United States and Canada,* 45–49.

———. "Snapshot: Jeans." *Encyclopedia of World Dress and Fashion,* Vol. 3, *The United States and Canada,* 64–65.

———. "Types and Properties of Fashionable Dress." *Encyclopedia of World Dress and Fashion,* Vol. 3, *The United States and Canada,* 63–67.

Tran, Khanh T. L. "Skate Brands Defy Gravity With Broader Reach." *WWD,* September 2, 2009. www.wwd.com/markets-news/skatewear-sector-shows-rapid-growth-2253642.

Trebay, Guy. "Roll Up Your Sleeves and Indulge in a Miami Vice." *New York Times,* July 20, 2006, www.nytimes.com/2006/07/20/fashion/20MIAMI.html?scp=2&sq=roll%20up%20your%20sleeves&st=cse (accessed May 13, 2011).

Usborne, David. "Charlie's timeless angels: Women who transformed television," *The Independent,* U.K., August. 30, 2006.

Valenti, Catherine. "Do Short Skirts Really Mean Better Times?" *ABC News,* January 17, 2003, http://abcnews.go.com/Business/story?id=86787&page=1.

Walker, Myra. "Cardin, Pierre." *The Berg Companion to Fashion,* ed. Valerie Steele. Oxford, U.K.: Berg, 2010, 116–118.

Ward, Susan. "Chemise Dress," *The Berg Companion to Fashion,* ed. Valerie Steele. Oxford, U.K.: Berg, 2010, 144–145.

Warner, Patricia. "Film." *Encyclopedia of World Dress and Fashion,* Vol. 3, *The United States and Canada,* ed. Phyllis G. Tortora. New York: Oxford University Press, 2010, 267–272.

Webber-Hanchett, Tiffany. "Bikini." *The Berg Companion to Fashion,* ed. Valerie Steele. Oxford, U.K.: Berg, 2010, 77–79.

Webber-Hanchett, Tiffany. "Madonna." *Encyclopedia of Clothing and Fashion.* Vol. 2, edited by Valerie Steele. New York: Charles Scribner's Sons, 2005, 370–372.

Welters, Linda. "The Beat Generation: Subcultural Style." *Twentieth-century American Fashion*, ed. Linda Welters and Patricia A. Cunningham. Oxford, UK: Berg, 2005, 145–167.

Welters, Linda, and Patricia A. Cunningham. "The Americanization of Fashion." *Twentieth-century American Fashion*, ed. Linda Welters and Patricia A. Cunningham, Oxford, U.K.: Berg, 2005, 1-8.

Wilson, Cintra. "You Just Can't Kill It." *New York Times*, September 17, 2008, www.nytimes.com/2008/09/18/fashion/18GOTH.html?scp=9&sq=Cintra%20Wilson&st=cse.

Wilson, Eric. "Macy's Gets Fast Fashion." *New York Times*, October 21, 2010, www.nytimes.com/2010/10/21/fashion/21ROW.html?scp=1&sq=Macy's%20Gets%20Fast%20Fashion&st=cse.

Winge, Therèsa. "Music and Dress in the United States." *Encyclopedia of World Dress and Fashion*, Vol. 3, *The United States and Canada*, ed. Phyllis G. Tortora. New York: Oxford University Press, 2010, 289–300.

Workman, Jane E., and Beth W. Freeburg. *Dress and Society*. New York: Fairchild; Oxford: Berg, 2009.

Worthington, Christa. "Keeping up with Kaiser Karl." *Women's Wear Daily*, February 21, 1986.

Young, William H. *The 1950s: American Popular Culture Through History*. Westport, CT: Greenwood Press, 2004.

Index

Page numbers in **boldface** are photographs.

About the Author

An award-winning writer/producer of corporate and educational media, **KAREN FRANKEL** has lived through most of the events, fashions, and fads described in *American Life and Fashion from Jeans to Jeggings*. She has also written *Projects About Ancient Rome* in the Hands-on History series. She graduated from Miami University in Oxford, Ohio, with a degree in history and has been an adjunct instructor at the Fashion Institute of Technology in New York City.